AF072126

We'll Live and Die in These Towns

To Sharon

My girl

We'll Live and Die in These Towns

Geoff Thompson

Copyright © Geoff Thompson 2018

All rights reserved

No part of this book may be reproduced by any means, nor transmitted, nor translated into a machine language without the written permission of the publisher.

ISBN 978-1-9164998-0-5

Printed and bound in Great Britain by 4edge Ltd.
Cover Design by the brilliant **Leigh Cunningham**
www.createonsight.co.uk

Note:
This play may not be performed without written permission from the publisher. Please contact the author through the Belgrade Theatre Coventry to discuss obtaining a licence to perform it.

Special thanks to:

Hamish Glen for his constant support

Joanna Reid for her generosity

Graham Baird, the best DSM in the business

Steve Cressy our wonderful Stage Manager

Amy-Marie Field our delightful ASM

Debbie O'Brien for doing such a great job with casting

Tom Clarke: this show could not have happened without Tom

Thank you to the incredible Liam Watts and Andy Hopkins of The Enemy, for their kind support on this project when I first approached them with it

John Dawkins, the former manager of The Enemy, who supported this project from the very start

Shameela Walker our lovely Assistant Director: I learned a lot from her about my own voice as a writer

Ray Clenshaw, Heather Kincaid, Shaista Hussain and all the lovely staff at the Belgrade, for brilliantly promoting our show

The lovely Linda at the ticket office, who is always so kind

My beautiful daughter Kerry for doing the first script edit for me

Where it has felt inspired I have either directly quoted from or lightly paraphrased some of the great works (and great men and women) that I have had the pleasure of reading. References to these tomes are scattered throughout the text like divine confetti: very specifically the Bhagavad-Gita upon which this story is based, more loosely the New Testament, the Torah, the Dhammapada, the Holy Koran, Milarepa, Rumi, Dante Alighieri, Reinhold Messner (Solo – Nanga Parbat) Paulo Coelho (The Alchemist), the Toa Te Ching, Abraham Maslow (Hierarchy of Needs), the lyrics of Tom Clarke are unashamedly referenced in order to weave our story into the songs, and lots of other beautiful, esoteric, obscure teachings that have greatly influenced me over the years, and that are now so much a part of my natural vernacular that I no longer know where I end and those essential scriptures begin.

The *quoted poem* on page 70 was taken from **Coventry**, by Ray Thompson.

Mostly this work came to me from the teacher-less instruction of Intuition, which inked the manna of our story on to the papyrus via visions and inspirations and intuitions.

I am very grateful to God for placing all of this knowing before me for our story.

The Belgrade Theatre Coventry Presents
We'll Live and Die in These Towns
By Geoff Thompson

Cast

Tom Milner	Argy
Andy Burse	Yudi/Sammy
Meg Forgan	Kusi/Megan
Adam Sopp	Matt/Danny
Quinn Patrick	Bill/Worker 1
Molly-Grace Cutler	Shelly/Brahma
Steven Serlin	Ambassador/Owl
Julie Mullins	Hips/Jane's Mum
Mark Turnbull	Busker/Worker 2

Creatives

Hamish Glen	Director
Geoff Thompson	Writer
Patrick Connellan	Designer
Tom Clarke	Musical Director
Chris Bogg	Sound Designer
Grant Anderson	Lighting Designer
Shanaz Gulzar	Videographer
Debbie O'Brien	Casting Director
Shameela Walker	Assistant Director

Production

Adrian Sweeney	Production Manager
Steve Cressy	Stage Manager
Graham Baird	Deputy Stage Manager
Amy-Marie Field	Assistant Stage Manager

Set and costume designs by Belgrade Productions Services
www.belgradeproductionservices.co.uk

Track list
Aggro
Pressure
Had Enough
Away From Here
You're Not Alone
It's Not Ok
40 Days and 40 Nights
We'll Live and Die in These Towns
This Song (partial)
This Song (full)
Technodanceaphobic
Aggro (partial)
40 Days and 40 Nights (full)
Canon
You're Not Alone
Happy Birthday Jane
Finale

We'll Live and Die in These Towns premiered at the Belgrade Theatre, Coventry from Sat 29 September 2018 in the B2 Auditorium.

Geoff Thompson

Geoff Thompson is a BAFTA Winning Writer.

Books

Geoff's first book, WATCH MY BACK, detailing his experiences as a doorman in Coventry for over a decade, became a *Sunday Times* Best Selling Autobiography. In 2008 it was adapted into a screenplay by Geoff and filmed as a major motion picture, CLUBBED. Geoff has written over forty books, and has been published in 21 languages. He has appeared three times on the *Sunday Times* Best Sellers List. He is also the author of myriad articles appearing in national magazines and broadsheets, including *The Times*, *GQ* and *FHM*.

Theatre

Geoff started his theatrical career when he was invited to join The Royal Court Young Writers Group.

His work as a playwright includes: **DOORMAN** (Liverpool Everyman, Plymouth Theatre Royal and National Tour); **FRAGILE** (Coventry Belgrade, Edinburgh Festival, King's Head Theatre London, Frankfurt, Berlin and a limited tour) **3 SACKS FULL OF HATS** (Finborough Theatre London, English Touring Theatre – rehearsed and private readings) and **THE PYRAMID TEXTS** (Birmingham Rep. and Soho Theatre, London). In 2015 Geoff work-shopped his play, **FOOD ORDER**, at The National Theatre Studio. Geoff's first musical for stage, **WE'LL LIVE AND DIE IN THESE TOWNS** (Dir. Hamish Glen/music and songs by Tom Clarke) premiered winter 2018 at the Belgrade Theatre Coventry.

We'll Live and Die in These Towns

Screenwriter

Short films
BOUNCER (dir. Michael Baig-Clifford) starring Ray Winstone and Paddy Considine, which was accepted into 32 international festivals and nominated for a BAFTA. **BROWN PAPER BAG** (dir. Michael Baig-Clifford) for which he was awarded a BAFTA. **PINK** (dir. Michael Baig-Clifford). **ROMANS 12:20** (dir. Shammasian brothers) which won Best Short at the Arpa International Film Festival, Best International Short Film New York International Independent Film & Video Festival, the Grand Prize at The Rhode Island International Film Festival, and the Long Form Award at Rushes Soho Shorts Festival. **COUNTING BACKWARDS** (dir. Sean de Sparengo) won Best Narrative Short at the Great Lakes Film Festival 2015, won Best Short Film category at the River Bend International Film Festival 2016 and was in Official Selection for Hamilton Film Festival 2015, Bronx International Film Festival 2016 and San Luis Obispo Film Festival 2016. **SHADOW** (2017) Official Selection: Hamilton Film Festival, Maryland International Film Festival, Fastnet Film Festival, Merit Award Winner Awareness Film Festival, Marbella International Film Festival (2018). **THE 20 MINUTE FILM PITCH** (dir. Steven Reynolds/Geoff Thompson) and **THREE SACKS FULL OF HATS** (dir. Debbie Anzalone), starring Alison Steadman and Warren Brown, in competition, Aesthetica Short Film Festival 2018 and Underwire Film Festival 2018.

Feature films
CLUBBED (dir. Neil Thompson) premiered in London's West End, Birmingham and Paris and was nominated for a BIFFA award for Best Film. **THE PYRAMID TEXTS** (dir. Shammasian

Geoff Thompson

Brothers), had its world premiere at The Edinburgh International Film Festival, 2015 and was nominated for The Michael Powell Award for Best British Film and won The Michael Powell Award for Best Actor in a British Film (James Cosmo). **ROMANS** (dir. Shammasian brothers) held its world premiere at the Edinburgh International Film Festival in 2017 and was nominated for The Michael Powell Award for Best British Film and won The Michael Powell Award for Best Actor in a British Film (Anne Reid). Geoff's fourth feature-film script for cinema, **ANIMAL DAY** (dir. Shammasian brothers) is currently optioned and in development with producer Ado Yoshizaki (NDF International) and the adaptation of his musical play, **WE'LL LIVE AND DIE IN THESE TOWNS**, has been optioned, and is in development with producer Lee Thomas (Prodigal Films).

Hamish Glen
Director

Hamish began his theatre career as a stage manager with the Traverse Theatre and Paines Plough, subsequently joining Shared Experience as assistant director. Following this, he formed the Writers Theatre Company, where he directed the British premieres of **At It** by Heathcote Williams and **More Happy Chickens** by Michael Duke. Working again with the Traverse Theatre, he directed the British premiere of Arthur Miller's **Two Way Mirror** and, as associate director of Tron Theatre, **The Overcoat** by Gogol, **Burning Love** by Kuse, **Gamblers** by Gogol, **Babes in the Wood** by Alan Cumming and Forbes Masson, and **The Tom and Sammy Show** by Peter Capaldi. Also: **As You Like It** and **Le Bourgeois gentilhomme** for the Royal Lyceum Theatre and **Gamblers** for the Lithuanian State Theatre.

We'll Live and Die in These Towns

As artistic director of Winged Horse Touring Productions, Hamish directed **The Magic Theatre** by John Clifford (after Cervantes), **Elizabeth Gordon Quinn** by Chris Hannan, **Bailegangaire** by Tom Murphy, **The Evil Doers** by Chris Hannan and **American Buffalo** by David Mamet.

Hamish was the artistic director at Dundee Rep from 1992–2003. His work there included: **Who's Afraid of Virginia Woolf?**, **Tartuffe**, **Uncle Vanya**, **The Hypochondriak**, **American Buffalo**, **Toshie** by Stuart Brown, **Death and the Maiden**, **Le Bourgeois gentilhomme**, **Cinderella** by Stuart Paterson, **Hyde** by Peter Arnott, **A Greater Tomorrow** by Hector MacMillan, **The Weavers** by Hauptmann, **The Mill Lavvies** by Chris Rattray and Michael Marra, **Puss in Boots** and **Hansel and Gretel**, both by Stuart Paterson. Hamish also directed **Walter** by C P Taylor, adapted by Michael Wilcox for the Edinburgh International Festival.

In 1999, Hamish launched a project called New Ways of Working at Dundee Rep that centred on the creation of a full-time ensemble company of 11 actors, and augmented each year by two apprentices. Hamish led them for the following four years, during which time he directed them in **Cabaret**, **Colquhoun and MacBryde** by John Byrne, **A Midsummer Night's Dream**, **A Family Affair**, **Measure for Measure** and **Nightflights** by Marcella Evaristi.

The ensemble regularly toured Scotland throughout its life and its success was recognised by the Scottish Theatre Awards in the first year they were set up, and a doubling of Scottish Arts Council funding 2003/04. This enabled the ensemble to become a permanent company. Other key successes of his artistic directorship was winning the Production of the Year TMA Award for **On the Line, A History of Timex in Dundee**, bringing Rimas Tuminas over from Lithuania to direct the ensemble in **The Seagull** in 2001 and taking Dundee Rep's production of **The Winter's Tale** to Iran in January 2003, where it won Best Foreign Production. **Hamish's work abroad includes: Gamblers** by Gogol for the Lithuanian State Theatre, **The Hypochondriak** for Mikkeli Theatre, Finland, which later transferred to the Tampere International Festival, **What the Butler Saw** for Tampere T Theatre and **A Delicate Balance** for Helsinki City Theatre.

Hamish became Artistic Director of the Belgrade Theatre, Coventry, in March 2003. **His Belgrade productions include: The Rink** by Kander and Ebb, a new adaptation of Molière's **The Hypochondriac**, Brecht's **Mr Puntila and His Man Matti, The Night Before Christmas**, Alan Pollock's play about the Coventry Blitz **One Night in November**, David Eldridge's new version of **Babylone, The Cheeky Chappies' Christmas Cracker**, David Johnston's adaptation of **The Miser**, Alan Pollock's play **Too Much Pressure, Stars in the Morning Sky** by Alexander Galin from an adaptation by Chris Hannan, Gogol's **Marriage, Propaganda Swing** by Peter Arnott**, The Sisterhood** by Ranjit Bolt and, most recently, he directed **The Quite Remarkable Adventures of the Owl and the Pussycat** and **Godiva Rocks**.

Tom Clarke
Musical Director

Tom was born in Birmingham in the mid 80's and moved to Coventry when he was in his teens. In 2006 after meeting

We'll Live and Die in These Towns

Liam Watts and Andy Hopkins, Tom formed **The Enemy**. The Enemy's' first Album **We'll Live and Die in These Towns** went straight to number one and quickly went platinum. Subsequent releases included three more top forty records, two of which were top ten, and to date have amassed sales well in excess of a million records. Since The Enemy's split Tom has opened a music venue in Coventry and embarked on several sell out solo acoustic tours. Tom is currently in the studio recording new material for a debut solo record.

Patrick Connellan
Designer

Theatre credits include: **Read All About It – City Final** and **Retold** (Co-Designer) (Belgrade Theatre site-specific production in Coventry Evening Telegraph building); **Whisky Galore** (Oldham Coliseum and national tour including Belgrade Theatre); **A Short History of Tractors in Ukrainian** (Hull Truck Theatre); **The Lion, the Witch and the Wardrobe** (Perm, Russia); **The Red Lion** (Olivier Award nominated) (Live Theatre, Newcastle and Trafalgar Studios, London); **Iris** (Live Theatre, Newcastle); **The Father** (Oldham Coliseum and Harrogate Theatre); **The Gaul** (Hull Truck Theatre); **The Baraem Play** (Costume Design) (Al Jazeera Media, Qatar); **The Hook** (Theatre Royal, Northampton and Liverpool Everyman); **The Ladykillers** (New Vic/Hull/Stephen Joseph); **Roll Over Beethoven, Three Minute Heroes, One Night in November, The Rink, A Midsummer Night's Dream, The Dice House, This Lime Tree Bower** (as Director and Designer, also Edinburgh Festival), **Silas Marner, She Stoops To Conquer, Leader of the Pack, Neville's Island, The Wedding** (Belgrade Theatre Coventry); **The Taming of the Shrew, The Merchant of**

Geoff Thompson

Venice and **Into the Woods** (nominated for TMA Best Musical Award) (Derby Theatre/Playhouse); **20th Century Boy** (New Wolsey); **Who's Afraid of Virginia Woolf, The Price, Ghosts, All My Sons, The Seafarer, Meet the Mukherjees, Popcorn** (also Director), **Broken Glass, Twelfth Night, Little Malcolm, The Weir** and **The Hypochondriac** (Octagon, Bolton); **Edward III** (RSC/West End); **A Passionate Woman, Misery** (West End); **The Slight Witch** (National Theatre/ Birmingham Rep); **Where Have I Been All My Life, Abigail's Party** (also Director) **Copenhagen** and **Alphabetical Order** (New Vic, Stoke) and for Hampstead Theatre: **Amongst Friends, Life After Scandal** (also Plymouth), **Taking Care of Baby** (also Birmingham Rep), **The Maths Tutor, Osama the Hero/A Single Act, My Best Friend** (also Birmingham Rep), **Nathan the Wise** and **When the Night Begins**. Credits for Birmingham Rep include: **Cider with Rosie** (also Holland Park Theatre) **The Grapes of Wrath, The Pied Piper, Pygmalion, Julius Caesar** and **Saint Joan**.

Patrick has previously won the Linbury Prize for Stage Design and a Prague Quadriennale Gold Medal. Patrick was the Course Leader for Theatre Design at Nottingham Trent University and is now a visiting lecturer in Theatre Design at the Royal Welsh College of Music and Drama, Cardiff.

Chris Bogg
Sound Designer

Christopher trained at Liverpool Institute for Performing Arts in Theatre and Performance Technology, graduating in 2003. He has designed for plays and musical theatre in the UK and abroad and has a passion for audio and for creating sound and music.

We'll Live and Die in These Towns

Theatre Sound Design Credits include: **Summer Holiday** (Bolton Octagon) **Pieces of String** World Premiere (Mercury Theatre Colchester) **Pippin** (Hope Mill Theatre), **Peter Pan** (Mercury Theatre Colchester), **Legally Blonde** (UK Tour), **Spamalot** (Mercury Theatre Colchester, UK Tour & Dubai), **Bring on the Bollywood** (UK Tour), **Yank** (European premiere, Hope Mill Theatre & London), **Wind In The Willows** (Mercury Theatre Colchester), **Hair** (Hope Mill Theatre), **End Of The Rainbow** (UK Tour), **Parade** (Hope Mill Theatre), **Avenue Q** (UK Tour & Hong Kong), **James And The Giant Peach** (International Tour), **Come Into The Garden** (BBC Philharmonic), **Seussical The Musical** (International Tour), **Little Red Riding Hood The Musical** (UK Premier, Pleasance London & Edinburgh), **Willemijn Verkaik** (Ambassadors Theatre), **Miracle on 34th Street The Musical** (UK Tour & Dubai), **Seussical The Musical** (Hong Kong), **Seussical** (Arts Theatre London), **Spring Awakening** (Kings Arms), **Christmas In New York** (Manchester Palace/Palace London), **Elements** (The Hammond Company, UK Tour), **The Kylie M Show** (UK Tour for Safi Productions), **911 Boy Band** (Official UK Tour 2014 & 2015).

Other Credits Include: **Katherine Jenkins** (UK Tour), **Spectacular Classics** (Raymond Gubbay, The Bridgewater Hall), **Space Classics** (Raymond Gubbay, The Bridgewater Hall), **Services No Longer Required** (BBC Philharmonic Orchestra, Imperial War Museum North), **Sinbad** (Ballet, World Premier, The Hammond Company), **Salford Tails** (BBC Philharmonic Orchestra, The Bridgewater Hall), **Wonder: A Scientific Oratorio** (World Premier, BBC Philharmonic Orchestra), **Fiddler On The Roof** (LIPA), **Scrooge The Musical** (BKL).

Geoff Thompson

Grant Anderson
Lighting Designer

Grant studied lighting design at The Royal Conservatoire of Scotland and graduated receiving the Dean of Drama Award for Best Individual Work.

Selected credits include: **Alan Cumming Sings Sappy Songs, Light on the Shore** (Edinburgh International Festival); **The Broons** national tour (Sell A Door); **Cuttin' A Rug, Simon's Magical Christmas Socks, Panic Patterns** (Citizens Theatre); **One Mississippi, Submarine Time Machine, To Begin** (National Theatre of Scotland & NTS Learn); **My Left Right Foot** (National Theatre of Scotland & Birds of Paradise); **Wendy Hoose, Blanch & Butch, The Tin Soldier** (Birds of Paradise); **A Christmas Carol, Love Song, In My Father's Words, Hecuba, Promises Promises, Baby Baby** (Dundee Repertory Theatre); **The Polar Bears Go Wild** (Macrobert, Stirling); **News Just In** (Random Accomplice); **And the Beat Goes On** (Perth Theatre & Random Accomplice); **Summer on Stage 2012 – 2016** (Lyceum Theatre); **The Maw Broon Monologues** (Tron Theatre); **Without a Hitch** (Room 2 Manoeuvre); **Chess, Into the Woods, Cabaret, 9 to 5, Urinetown, Addams Family, Godspell, Avenue Q, Sunday in the Park With George, Company, Women on the Verge of a Nervous Breakdown, Wasted Love, Show Choir** (Royal Conservatoire of Scotland); **Little Red and the Wolf, Freak Show, Forest Boy, The Girl Who** (Noisemaker); **Barnum, Les Miserables, Godspell, Annie, Guys & Dolls, Just So, Once On This Island, 13, Seussical, Ragtime** (Forth Children's Theatre) and **A Clockwork Orange** (associate, Theatre Royal Stratford East).

Grant has also designed extensively for the Events Industry, including **Botanic Lights 2015 Seasons in Colour** and 2016 **EXPLORE,** (Royal Botanic Garden Edinburgh); **Edinburgh's Hogmanay Torchlight Procession & Street Party**, including the 2017 Midnight Moment. Grant was also responsible for designing Scotland's *2014* **Moment Edinburgh**. As well as designing in the UK, Grant's work has transferred internationally to New York, Beijing, Madrid, Valencia and Rio de Janeiro.

Shanaz Gulzar
Videographer

Shanaz is a digital installation artist and stage designer who also works as a producer on specialist projects. Her work explores interactions between new technologies, film, theatre, place and identity and she is known for creating work across disciplines to make innovative and challenging interventions. She has a clear and distinct artistic voice with a vision for producing ambitious, contemporary art that is accessible to both arts and none arts audiences.

Shanaz's recent works include: **Veil**, immersive installation and performance space for spoken word exploring the hijab; **United Colours of FrustrAsian** (Cast Doncaster, Part of The Alchemy Festival on Tour 2015, The Southbank); **Who's Saree Now?** (Rasa Productions); **Made in India** (Tamasha Theatre); **HOME1947** (Producer, Manchester International Festival with double Oscar winning film maker Sharmeen Obald Chinoy); **Calderland** (509 Arts Outdoor site specific Community Opera at The Piece Hall Halifax); **Sisters** (National Theatre Wales) and **Read All About It!** (Belgrade Theatre Coventry).

Geoff Thompson

Current works include: **Different from What We Are** (VR narrative based installation with ARC Stockton and Eclipse Theatre); **Tide Whisperer** (Live stream Film Director, National Theatre Wales) and **Producer for Manchester** International Festival 2019.

Debbie O'Brien
Casting Director

West End productions include: **Thriller Live; The Knowledge;** Dirty Dancing; The Rat Pack Live from Las Vegas; Close to You; Sinatra; American Idiot; Dusty; In the Bar of a Tokyo Hotel; Priscilla Queen of the Desert; Grease; Flashdance; Piaf; The Snowman; Respect La Diva; The King and I; The Harder They Come; Showboat; Dancing in the Streets; Chitty Chitty Bang Bang; Saturday Night Fever; Fame; Peter Pan; The Pirates of Penzance; Mum's the Word; Daisy Pulls It Off; Napoleon; Madame Melville; Hedwig and the Angry Inch; La Cava; Smokey Joe's Café; The Rocky Horror Show; Soul Train; Rent; Always; Steaming; Ain't Misbehavin' and Disgracefully Yours.

Children's casting includes: **Caroline or Change; Annie; Kinky Boots; The Bodyguard; Show Boat; The Sound of Music.**

UK tours include: 20th Century Boy; Our House; Grease; Laila; a new Musical; Jackie the Musical; Let It Be; Mum's the Word; So This Is Christmas; Footloose; American Idiot; Priscilla Queen of the Desert; Crush the Musical; Thriller Live; The Bodyguard and Annie (children's casting); Dancing in the Streets; The Threepenny Opera; Soul Sister; I Was a Rat; Carnaby Street; Dreamboats and Petticoats;

We'll Live and Die in These Towns

Flamenco Flamen'ka; Burn the Floor; 51 Shades of Maggie; Doctor In the House; Hormonal Housewives; Tell Me On a Sunday; Cacophony; Menopause the Musical; Flashdance; Defending the Caveman; The Rat Pack Live From Las Vegas; Mahabharata; Sweet Soul Music; Starlight Express; Anything Goes; What a Feeling; Dirty Dusting; Mack and Mabel; The Misanthrope; A Chorus Line; A Tribute to the Blues Brothers; Smokey Joe's Cafe; The Rocky Horror Show; Soul Train and Wild Animus.

Other London; regional and international productions include: Once the Musical; Jersey Boys, After Midnight, Rock of Ages, The Choir of Man, Priscilla Queen of the Desert (all NCL); We Live and Die In These Towns; Starlight Express (Bochum and international tour) Oxy and the Morons; Room; Godiva Rocks; Snow White; The Last Five Years; Ostrich Boys; The Burnt Part Boys; Red Snapper; The Sisterhood; Only a Day; Cougar; Medea; Much Ado About Nothing; As You Like It; A Midsummer Night's Dream; Romeo and Juliet; The Comedy of Errors; Merry Wives of Windsor and Twelfth Night; Noises Off; And Then the Dark; The Bubbly Black Girl Sheds Her Chameleon Skin; Treasure Island; Five Guys Named Moe; Kiss Me Kate; Top Hat; West Side Story; Thoroughly Modern Millie; Singing in the Rain; Legally Blonde; Cats (RCCL); Midsummer Songs; The BFG; Evolution; South Pacific; Sister Act; Jackie the Musical; Hairspray; Fame; Alice in Wonderland; The Sound of Music; Chicago; Hair; The Opera Show; Soul Sister; Little Shop of Horrors; The Corstorphine Road Nativity; White Christmas; Mods and Rox; Robin Hood; It's a Wonderful Life; Laurel and Hardy; Blues in the Night; My Fair Lady; Anything Goes; The Sound of Music; Me and My Girl; Little Shop of Horrors; Guys and Dolls;

Geoff Thompson

Crazy For You; Oklahoma!; The Opera Show; The Pirates of Penzance; The Wizard of Oz; Motherhood the Musical; Amadeus; The Snowman; Side by Side by Sondheim; Only You Can Save Mankind and 100% Sex Therapy.

Recorded media: **Waybuloo**; **Grandpa in My Pocket**; **What's Your News?**; **Buddy Patrol**; **Tic Toc**; **Quick Quack Duck**; **Grease is the Word**; **How Do You Solve a Problem Like Maria**; **Amahl and the Night Visitors**; **Planet Cook** and Energy.

Tom Milner
Argy

Tom is originally from West Yorkshire and is well known for playing series regular Paul Langley in the BBC drama **Waterloo Road**. He was also a contestant on **The Voice** (BBC) in Ricky Wilson's team and is a regular guest artist with The Barricade Boys. Further Television & Film credits include **Starlings** (Sky 1); **Holby City** and **Doctors** (BBC); **Barking** (CITV) and **Plastic The Movie**.

Tom's stage credits include: **Cinderella** (Southport Theatre); **Dick Whittington** (City Varieties Music Hall); **Waterbabies** (Curve Theatre); **Jack and the Beanstalk** (Charter Theatre); **Cinderella** (Charter Theatre); **Soho Cinders** (Soho Theatre) and **Sleeping Beauty** (Victoria Theatre).

In 2019, he'll play the lead role of Johnny in the 10th Anniversary cast of American Idiot (UK tour).

Twitter: @tomkmilner

We'll Live and Die in These Towns

Andy Burse
Yudi/Sammy

Theatre credits include: **Treasure Island** (New Vic Theatre); **Out Of The Shadows** (Nuffield Theatre); **The Lock-In** (Over the Limit); **Wojtek: The Happy Warrior** (Quarter Too Ensemble); *Cat Ninelives* (Walking Forward); **Tuesday** (Upstairs At Three And Ten); **Henry V** (Minerva Theatre, Chichester); **Tiny Tempest** (MiniMall); **Uncle Montague's Stories From the Shadows, The Comedy of Errors, Antigone, A Respectable Wedding, Private Peaceful** (OnO Theatre) and **Romeo and Juliet** (Sussex Actors Studio).

Film credits include: **On Chesil Beach** (Number 9 Films).
Television credits include: **Guiltology** (Nutopia Limited).
Radio credits include: *Riot Girls* (BBC Radio).
Andy graduated from Rose Bruford in 2016. Theatre at Rose Bruford include: **The Cane; Urinetown: The Musical; Egor Bulychev and the Others; Henry V; Attempts on her Life; My Marriage Is…** and **Orpheus Descending**.

Meg Forgan
Kusi/Megan

Meg Forgan has recently graduated from the Royal Conservatoire of Scotland.

We'll Live and Die in These Towns will be her professional debut since graduating.

Credits whilst training include: **London Road** (Royal Conservatoire of Scotland); **Spring Awakening** (Royal

Conservatoire of Scotland/Dundee Rep); **Sideshow** (Royal Conservatoire of Scotland); **Candid Cabarets** (Royal Conservatoire of Scotland) and **The Coolidge Effect** (UK TOUR).

Adam Sopp
Matt/Danny

Adam's Theatre credits include: **OV200** (Old Vic); **The Dog Beneath The Skin** (Jermyn Street); **946: The Amazing Story of Adolphus Tips** (Kneehigh & Shakespeare's Globe/US tour); **Sunny Afternoon** (Hampstead Theatre/West End); **Symphony** (Nabokov/Waterloo Vaults); **The El Train** (Hoxton Hall); **Backbeat** (West End/US Tour); **The Daughter In Law** (New Vic), **A Chorus of Disapproval** (New Wolsey/Mercury) and **All Quiet On The Western Front** (Nottingham Playhouse).

Television credits include: **Call The Midwife, Casualty, Holby City, Doctors, Father Brown, WPC 56** and **Grange Hill** (BBC); **Stan Lee's Lucky Man** and **The Lost Honour of Christopher Jefferies** (Carnival Films) and **Casualty 1907** (Stone City Films).

Film credits include: **Abroad** (Big Tree Productions) and **Expectation Management** (Independent Content).

Quinn Patrick
Bill/Worker 1

Theatre credits include: **The Wind in the Willows** (Image Theatre Co.); **Arsenic and Old Lace** (Kenneth Wax Productions and Nick Brooke ltd); **Bouncers** (Bruce James Productions);

We'll Live and Die in These Towns

Lucky Sods (Bruce James Productions); **Funny Money** (Bruce James Productions); **I'll Be Back Before Midnight; Kindly Keep It Covered**. Musical roles include **Little Shop of Horrors** (Bruce James Productions); **Grand Central** (Anthony Day) and **Bananaman The Musical** (Sightline Productions). Quinn has a wealth of pantomime experience, and for many years has performed as the traditional pantomime dame, in theatres throughout the UK.

Television credits include **Without Motive** (Alibi Productions), **Castoffs** (Eleven Films & CH4) and **Moving On, Casualty, Shakespeare and Hathaway** (BBC Television). Most recently Quinn filmed a special episode of the hit TV show **Trollied** (Sky One and Roughcut TV). He appeared in BAFTA winning children's TV shows **Grandpa In My Pocket** (Adastra/BBC) and global hit **HaHa Hairies** (Adastra/Cartoon Network/SC4).

Films include **Elevator Gods** (Happy Our Films) **Danny and the Human Zoo** (BBC Film and Red Productions), and **Mariachi** (HSI London).

Quinn can also be seen on the stand-up circuit. He debuted his own one-man comedy show **Shut your Cakehole** at The Edinburgh Festival and has since enjoyed sell out London shows.

Molly-Grace Cutler
Brahma and Shelly

Molly-Grace trained at the Mountview Academy of Theatre Arts.

Geoff Thompson

Her theatre credits include: **Priscilla Queen if The Desert** (Queen's Theatre, Hornchurch); **Beauty and The Beast** (Queen's Theatre, Hornchurch) and **Oxy and The Morons** (New Wolsey Theatre, Ipswich).

TV credits include: **Timewasters** (ITV2 and Big Talk Productions)

Steven Serlin
Ambassador/Owl

Steven has recently finished playing the role of Ali Hakim in Grange Park Opera's production of **Oklahoma**.

He has had a varied career in the world of Theatre. Roles include Monty in the West End and UK Touring productions of **Saturday Night Fever**, Angelo in Sir Peter Hall's West End production of **Piaf**, The Dentist in **Little Shop of Horrors** and Goldberg in **The Wild Party** which opened the Other Palace Theatre in London.

Other Theatre Credits include: **Jack and the Beanstalk** (Salisbury Playhouse); **Charlie and the Chocolate Factory** (Theatre Royal, Drury Lane); **I Can't Sing** (The London Palladium); **The Infidel** (Stratford East); **Mack and Mabel** (Southwark Playhouse); **Peter Pan** (Waterside, Aylesbury); **Imagine This** (New London); **Monkee Business** (UK Tour); **Company** (Southwark Playhouse); **Arsenic and Old Lace** (Salisbury Playhouse); **Our House** (UK Tour); **Chess The Concert** (Royal Albert Hall); **Desperately Seeking Susan** (West End); **Treasure Island** (Lincoln Theatre Royal); Boogie Nights (West End and Tour); **Grease** (Dominion); **Scrooge The**

We'll Live and Die in These Towns

Musical (UK Tour); **Godspell** (Rep); **The Rocky Horror Show** (Tour); **Elvis the Musical** (Tour); **Popcorn** (Rep); **Ken Hill's Zorro** (Theatre Royal Stratford East); **A Slice Of Saturday Night** (Tour); Jesus Christ Superstar (25th Anniversary Tour); **Bedroom Farce** (Rep); **Chess** (1st National Tour); **Joseph and his Amazing Technicoloured Dreamcoat** (Tour); **Copacabana** (Tour) and **The Rise and Fall of Little Voice** (Rep).

Television Includes: **Frank Stubbs Promotes; Inspector Poirot; Casualty; Royal Variety Show** and Eugenius in the Short Film **Musical Star.**

Julie Mullins
Hips/Jane's Mum

Television includes: Julie Martin (nee Robinson) in **Neighbours** (The Grundy Organization); Mary Quinn in **Land of Hope** (JNP Films & Channel 7, Australia); **A Country Practice** (Channel 7, Australia); **Palace of Dreams** (ABC, Australia); **Wild and Wooley** (ABC, Australia) and Butterfly Island (Independent Films, Australia).

Theatre incudes: Julie Mullins One Woman Show in **All the Girls You Are!** (The Pheasantry, London); **Body to Diet For** (Etcetera & Landor Theatres, London); **The Expat Wife** (Singapore & Hong Kong Tour); **As You Like It** (The Acting Factory, Australia); **Much Ado About Nothing** (The Acting Factory, Australia); **They're Playing Our Song** (Asian & Middle Eastern Tour); **Dearly Beloved** (Bridewell Theatre, London); **Triumphs and Mirth** (Shakespeare's Globe, London); **They're Playing Our Song** (Haymarket Theatre, Basingstoke); **Sleeping Beauty** (Theatre Royal, Bath); **Babes in the Wood**

(Sadlers Wells Theatre, London); **Return to the Forbidden Planet** (Australian Tour); **Anything Goes** (Australian & New Zealand Tour); **Hating Alison Ashley** (Theatre South, NSW & Victorian Tour); **True Patriots All** (Q Theatre, Australia); **Tarantara Tarantara** (Q Theatre, Australia); **The Sentimental Bloke** (Melbourne Theatre Company & Victorian Tour); **The Hostage** (Q Theatre, Australia) and
The Mathemagician (Toe Truck Theatre Company, NSW Tour).

Web Series includes: Neighbours vs Time Travel (Freemantle Media).

Cabaret includes: **As Time Goes By** (Joan Sutherland Performing Arts Centre, Australia); **Julie Mullins Quartet** (Italy); **Julie Mullins Quintet** (Ireland); **Love That Many Splendored Thing** (Norfolk, UK); **Julie Sings Judy Garland** (Mietta's Cabaret Lounge, Australia) and **Julie Sings** (Prior Engagements, Australia).

Workshop incudes: **Ida Rubenstein** (The Playground Theatre, London) and **The Big Smoke** (Playbox Theatre, Australia).

Mark Turnbull
Busker/Worker 2

Trained at: Webber Douglas Academy and Rose Bruford College (MA in Theatre and Performance).

Theatre credits include: **Aladdin** (Crewe Lyceum), **The Man Who Had All the Luck** (King's Head Theatre); **The Goodbye Girl** (Upstairs at the Gatehouse); **How to Succeed in Business**

We'll Live and Die in These Towns

Without Really Trying (Ye Olde Rose and Crown); **Marguerite** directed by Guy Unsworth; **Jekyll and Hyde** (Morphic Graffiti); **Billy, The Baker's Wife** (Union Theatre); **Chicago, Jesus Christ Superstar, Guys and Dolls, Annie Get Your Gun, The Rocky Horror Show** (UK tours and abroad); **Les Misérables** (Palace Theatre) and **The Rocky Horror Show** (Piccadilly Theatre).

Cabaret credits include: solo cabaret of Sondheim Songs, **I'm Still Here** (Ye Old Rose and Crown).

Preface

Just three days before we started auditions for **We'll Live and Die in These Towns**, with the lovely casting director Debbie O'Brien in London, I suffered a spiritual crisis. Perhaps *crisis* is too strong a word, it was more of a spiritual wobble. My faith in God was not threatened, only faith in my ability to hear His direction felt compromised. We were in pre-production with a film that I had been working on for five years. We were due to shoot in three weeks' time when the lead actor suddenly and inexplicably pulled out. It left me and the whole crew in a vulnerable limbo. We'd had all pretty much worked on spec with this project, as well as the satisfaction of seeing the film acted and directed and finally on screen, we were all looking forward to finally getting paid, actually we were all desperate to get paid – it had been a long time between drinks. When our actor pulled out – the second time he had done this – the film collapsed and it felt like the five years of work was all for nothing. For the first time in many years I doubted my path as a dramatist, as a man whose covenant with God was to tell stories that might act as an intercession for people lost or in pain or suffering the vicissitudes of life.

Was this really my path?

Was this really where God wanted me to be?

I love to write, I feel it is my dharma find a page for the words that come to me. Writing is my raison d'être but, be in no doubt, if I felt *even for a second* that it was not where God wanted me, I would drop it like a bad habit.

We'll Live and Die in These Towns

I have a great faith in God, and when I work in His alignment, He always provides the wherewithal – the basic necessities, the roof, the means of movement, *supper* – to sustain my work. When it felt as though the divine funding was suddenly withdrawn I questioned my path. For the first time in living memory I wobbled and I asked my mum, 'do you think this is where God wants me to be, because our film has just disappeared and I don't understand why?' My lovely mum teared up: 'If God wants you to be somewhere else son, He will tell you soon enough, don't you worry about that.'

I did what I always do when I fall into doubt, I went straight to God, in my prayers, 'am I on the right path?' I asked.

It was later that week, in a small community hall in London – our casting location for this play, sitting with the director Hamish Glen, and the musical director Tom Clarke, that I was given my answer.

Every fifteen minutes for three days, we saw a different person auditioning for one of the nine parts in our story, and every fifteen minutes for three days I was given the answer to my question: *'yes, yes, yes. This is the right path for you, this is where God wants you.'*

It was one of the most spiritually uplifting times of my life, actors young and old, presented themselves to us in the most beautifully abandoned and utterly professional manner. Their auditions were so naked, and so uncompromised and enchanting they filled the room with joy.

Geoff Thompson

The very first person to audition on day one set a very high bar. She was a young, beautiful and enigmatic woman called Meg Forgan. She still hadn't graduated yet from the Royal Conservatoire of Scotland, and had travelled all the way from Glasgow just for this audition. She blew us all away. No exaggeration needed. I knew the moment she started to sing that she would be cast in the play. She was followed by a banquet of amazing talent; the brilliant Tom Milner awed us not just with his voice but also with his humility and his willingness to learn and to stretch, he *was* our lead, Argy: Steven Serlin had everyone in hysterics when he lifted the characters *Ambassador* and *Owl* from the dry page and made them real before our eyes, he was so good I kissed him afterwards: the beautiful Quinn Patrick was sensitive and subtle and deeply seasoned in his audition for the parts of Bill and Worker 1 – the room went still every time he spoke: the brilliant Molly Grace Cutler, having only looked at the script the night before walked onto the stage and she *was* Shelly, she clothed our creation with blood and bone and sinew; the moment she started to act, we all knew she was our girl: the veteran actor and West End star Mark Turnbull, met every dimension (and added some of his own) for *Busker*, he was so steady, he exuded experience, such an erudite man, just his presence in the room, inspired me to add new aspects (and a stuffed dog) to the script: the musical genius of Adam Sopp and Andy Burse left the whole audition panel in no doubt that they would be our first choices in the roles of Danny and Sammy, and as if to top the three days off with a big Australian cherry, the very classy Julie Mullins took the boards and had everyone in the room crying, when she sang for the parts of Hips and Jane's Mum.

We'll Live and Die in These Towns

If I had any doubts about where I was meant to be, they were dismissed immediately in the audition process, and that dismissal was capitalised upon in the rehearsals, which were an exhausting, exhilarating delight.

I got the chance to work for the first time in the rehearsal room with Artistic Director Hamish Glen. It was an inspiration for me; I was witness to moments of quiet genius, as this brilliant man shaped words on a page into a play, fit for the stage at the Belgrade theatre, Coventry.

I was also back in the room again with my beautiful friend Graham Baird, our DSM, I had worked closely with him before on a play at the Belgrade called Fragile: I loved working with him then, I loved it again now: he always looks after me. To top it all off, I got to work with Tom Clarke, our MD and former front man to The Enemy, upon whose debut album We'll Live and Die in These Towns, is based.

If you were a Beatles fan, this would be like sitting with John Lennon or Paul McCartney, while they played guitar and wrote music and sang.

I am a big Enemy fan, and I got to sit in the room with Tom Clarke, whilst he weaved his magic. I am not sure if it can ever get any better than that.

I was on the right path. I *am* on the right path. Of that I *am* certain.

Foreword

The idea for this musical was birthed in a small private gymnasium, at the back of my house in Coventry, where I push weights, practice yoga and listen to inspirational tunes.

My taste in music is eclectic; I like anything from Leonard Cohen to Bob Dylan, Hans Zimmer to Moby, but the music I listened to most during my gladiatorial anti-gravity work-outs was The Enemy – specifically their breakthrough, million-selling album **We'll Live and Die in These Towns**.

The Enemy were my training mainstay for many years.

It was while listening to the rawness and the poetry and the punk of Tom Clarke's brilliant music and lyrics, that I had an inspiration: *these songs would work beautifully in a stage musical.*

The arc of the album tells its own story and it is a tale that is as old as time. It speaks of class discrimination, negative conditioning and mans need for purpose.

To carry the songs through a two-hour stage play that is worthy of the Belgrade Theatre, I needed a story with gravitas, one that was not only historical in its message, but also universal in its theme.

I didn't want to limit the play to a biopic, nor write a commentary on the life of a specific person or band, so whilst our story finds its inspiration in the songs of The Enemy, and enjoys the blessing of the band themselves, I was free to let the story take me wherever it was best served.

We'll Live and Die in These Towns

As serendipity would have it, I am a great lover of ancient texts, and there can be few that inspire the imagination more than the Hindu classics. Known in theosophical circles as *the fruit of the Vedas*, The Bhagavad-Gita consists of 18 chapters, and 700 slokas: this, the reduction of 500,000 Vedic verses that date back several millennia before the birth of Christianity.

The Gita tells the story of a Prince (Arjuna Pandava) who enters the theatre of war (in order to win back his stolen kingdom) only to lose heart the moment he alights on the field of battle. As well as the enemy soldiers, Arjuna also encounters in the fighting ranks his father figures, his friends, his uncles, his teachers, his cousins and his brothers. As soon as he sees them, his courage fails, and he decides that he can't fight; he would rather become a renunciant, he would sooner roam the forests begging for food, than win a kingdom at the cost of his family.

His companion on the chariot of war is Lord Krishna, the Godhead. Seeing his friend's distress, he delivers a spiritual discourse (the Gita) that helps realign Arjuna to his true purpose, and allows him to enter the fight and win back his throne.

The Gita offers an incredibly powerful allegory about humanities battle with fear, and the mortal wrestle most of us have on a daily basis with the false beliefs (or false news) that lead us into war; locally, in the daily microcosm of our minds, and non-locally in the perennial macrocosm of the world at large.

This was the inspiration I used for my play, but with a contemporary slant. Our antagonist, Argy is not a reluctant prince, fearful to enter the fight, rather he is a burgeoning rock star who suffers debilitating stage-fright, hours before the biggest performance of his life.

Argy is afraid, he fears that if he takes the stage, he will be abandoning his family, selling out his friends, eschewing his class; all he wants to do is go back to playing the pubs and clubs, where he was accepted, where he felt safe.

His manager, unable to talk him down, gives him twenty-four hours to re-visit his past, to contemplate the present, and decide his future.

Even though our story is my own personal take on the original, its message remains intact, and it is as important today as it was all those thousands of years ago, when it first left the pen of the sages and priests of lore.

We'll Live and Die in These Towns (the album) is ten years old at the writing of this book, but the lyrics about personal freedom, the fight for equality and class discrimination are timeless.

Ours is an age of reality TV. People are being humiliated for entertainment, seduced into the televisual coliseum by the lure of fast fame. They are betting their souls for (the promise of) material fortune, societal approval and vacuous applause: but the house always wins.

If there was ever a time for an inspirational discourse that helps realign people to their true purpose, it is now.

PART 1

Darkness

We hear the opening bars of 'Aggro.'

Out of the darkness:

ARGY (*sings*). Call the police!

Lights up.

We are in a rehearsal room.
*On the wall there is a sign...**The Throne Room Arena.***
ARGY (sporting a trendy cap*) is on the mic and lead guitar.*
His band **KURU KINGDOM** *include:*
YUDI THIRA is on the drums.
MATT VADA is on piano.
KUSI is on the bass.
BRAHMA is on the electric guitar.

Their manager, THE AMBASSADOR *is on the sidelines watching.*

ARGY *sings* 'Aggro'.

Aggro
https://www.youtube.com/watch?v=Ct7FuFI9KzQ

ARGY
Cos things are getting ugly
Get on your feet,

We'll Live and Die in These Towns

I want you running with me
Do what you like,
Say what you mean
Do what you please
Ahhhhh we'll set the streets on fire
And when it comes on top
We'll give it lots of aggro
Were giving it lots of aggro
Ahhhhh we'll set the streets on fire
And when it comes on top
We'll give it lots of aggro
Were giving it lots of aggro
Blood on the streets,
You see the trouble happening
Get on your feet,
You see the crowds are gathering
Do what you like,
Say what you mean
Do what you please
Ahhhhh we'll set the streets on fire
And when it comes on top
We'll give it lots of aggro
Were giving it lots of aggro
Ahhhhh we'll set the streets on fire
And when it comes on top
We'll give it lots of aggro
Were giving it lots of aggro
Ahhhhh we'll set the streets on fire
And when it comes on top
We'll give it lots of aggro
Were giving it lots of aggro
Ahhhhh we'll set the streets on fire

And when it comes on top
We'll give it lots of aggro
Were giving it lots of aggro

THE AMBASSADOR *claps his hands.*
He looks delighted.

THE AMBASSADOR. Brilliant! Brilliant, brilliant, brilliant. You're going to smash it. You... are going to kill it (to *the band*), rest your weapons. Argy over here with me.

The band relax.

ARGY *walks over to* THE AMBASSADOR, *still carrying his guitar.*

THE AMBASSADOR. So how you feeling? Excited? Nervous, thrilled!
ARGY. I'm raring.
THE AMBASSADOR. What the matter with your face (*pinches* ARGY'S *face cheeks*), you're as pale as a Russian swimmer.
ARGY. Adrenalin. It's all right. I've got it.
THE AMBASSADOR. Your legs look like they're doing an involuntary bossanova.
ARGY (*laughs*). What legs! I've lost all the feeling below my waist.
THE AMBASSADOR. Legs are overrated as far as I'm concerned. As long as you don't fall over on that stage, you'll be dandy.
ARGY. Bit of nerves – it's all good. It'll fire me up.
THE AMBASSADOR. Spikes the *claret* kid, kicks the blood round your veins like a demented bob-slay.

ARGY (*whoops/claps hands together hard*). WHOOOO – I'm ready.

THE AMBASSADOR. There are 20,000 tickets out there, waiting to hear your song.

ARGY. That's a football crowd.

THE AMBASSADOR. It *is* a football crowd! (Indicates all around him) This is The Throne Room kid. One of the greatest rock arenas on this spinning planet. And they've come to see you.

ARGY. Take me to the stage. I want to see who's in.

THE AMBASSADOR walks ARGY stage left.
They stop at a door marked **STAGE DOOR**.
THE AMBASSADOR holds the door handle.
He winks at ARGY

THE AMBASSADOR. This...is the gateless gate (*off AGY'S confusion*). It is a mysterious doorway, the portal to a different dimension, a new reality: it keeps the unworthy out, it lets the worthy in.

ARGY *nods*.

Sure you're ready for this?
ARGY. I'm OK to go.

THE AMBASSADOR opens the stage door just a crack.
The roar of the thousands is cacophonous.
It literally blows the cap off ARGY'S *head like a rogue wind.*
ARGY *makes an audible gasp.*
Mysteriously the same gust leaves THE AMBASSADOR *untouched.*

THE AMBASSADOR. Makes your breath go faster, don't it kiddo.

ARGY *does not respond.*
He is frozen to the spot with fear.
THE AMBASSADOR *is staring out at the amassing crowd.*
He is oblivious to ARGY's *growing terror.*
ARGY'S *guitar slips though his fingers.*
The body of the instrument clunks on the floor.
ARGY *looks at his shaking fingers.*
It is as though he has lost control of his hands.

ARGY *(he rubs his stomach)*. I feel funny. My belly's going like a brass band.
THE AMBASSADOR. It's natural. It's a big gig ain't it. You're sharing space with some weighty songs: Oasis. Kasabian. Stereophonics. The Preachers. *(Mimics Mick Jagger)* I've just had a piss next to Mick and Keith.

ARGY *looks as though he might faint.*
ARGY *turns toward the audience.*
We hear his next words **off stage** *(as a voice over).*
We are hearing ARGY'S *most private thoughts and fears,*
When THE AMBASSADOR *speaks we are aware that* ARGY *is not hearing him.*
Likewise, THE AMBASSADOR *is completely oblivious to* ARGY'S *state.*
Two dialogues, concurrent but disparate.
ARGY *is at the beginning of a full-blown panic attack.*

ARGY *(Off: deep breath/struggling)*. Ohhhh. My breath. My breath is gone. Can't breathe.

THE AMBASSADOR. After the show – while I think about it – interviews:

ARGY (*off*). My heart is kicking out of my chest.

THE AMBASSADOR. The music press are in –

ARGY (*off*). I feel dizzy.

THE AMBASSADOR. The tabloids, the broad sheets –

ARGY (*off*). My fingers are numb...

THE AMBASSADOR. Local TV, national TV, Sky News –

ARGY (*Off: wipes brow/dripping sweat*). Sweating...what's happening to me...?

THE AMBASSADOR. Local radio, Radio 4, Radio 1 –

ARGY (*Off*). My tongue is tingling...

THE AMBASSADOR. There are 20 *on-line heavy-weights* with a *monster* following –

ARGY (*Off*). I've got to get out of here: I've got to go...

THE AMBASSADOR. We've got a flurry of back-to-backs for gossip mags and red-tops and blogs and pod-casts –

ARGY (*off*). My chest is *tight* –

THE AMBASSADOR. There's Twitter –

ARGY (*off*). I'm having a stroke...

THE AMBASSADOR. There's Facebook –

ARGY (*off*). My heart is attacking me –

THE AMBASSADOR. There's Instagram –

ARGY (*off*). *I'm dying.*

THE AMBASSADOR. The NME are in the building!

ARGY (*Off*). I'm dying, I'm dying, I'm dying, I'm dying ...

THE AMBASSADOR. They all want to know what you had for breakfast this morning, they all want to know what you think about the starving millions in the third world –

ARGY (*off*). I'm dying...

THE AMBASSADOR. Tell them that you eat like there's a famine and you are personally going to visit the

disenfranchised at your earliest convenience: you'll feed the starving by hand if you have to.
ARGY (*screams, on 'have to'*). I'M DYING!!!!

THE AMBASSADOR *stops in his tracks.*
He suddenly notices ARGY *sitting on the floor, in a nervous state.*

THE AMBASSADOR (*shocked*). What the? Are you all right? What happened? Did you fall?
ARGY. My heart....
THE AMBASSADOR. What about your heart?
ARGY. My throat...I can't...something's...can't swallow...

THE AMBASSADOR *forces* ARGY's *mouth open.*

THE AMBASSDOR. Let's have a look (*looks*) nothing! Have you...you had enough water?

THE AMBASSADOR *tries to stand him.*

Let's get you standing.

ARGY *flops back down, limp.*

ARGY. Can't breathe, can't breathe...

THE AMBASSADOR *grabs* ARGY *stands him up again.*

THE AMBASSADOR. Let's get you walking.

ARGY *flops again; a rag.*

ARGY. My legs are gone...my tongue...my tongue is numb –

THE AMBASSADOR *is getting more and more panicked.*

Can't swallow...I'm dying, I think I'm dying –

ARGY *starts to hyperventilate, he panics.*

THE AMBASSADOR. Medic! Medic.

ARGY *flops over into a lying position, half unconscious.*

THE AMBASSADOR (*Screams*). MEDIC!

A lighting change.

First Aid room.

Two plastic chairs.
ARGY *is sat on one of the chairs, towel around his neck looking pale.*
THE AMBASSADOR *is standing away from* ARGY.
THE AMBASSADOR *is pacing, his hands in his pockets.*
He looks at his watch, perplexed.

THE AMBASSADOR. How you feeling. You feeling any better?

ARGY *nods.*

Had me bloody worried for a minute there...I thought I was going to have to do my CPR on you; *m' first aid*. I thought you was having a heart failure.

ARGY *nods.*
He did too.

(*Incredulous*) Panic attack!

ARGY *is a little sheepish.*

Flipping...panic attack – I mean...I didn't know they were real, I thought *panic attack* was an American grunge band. Why...Argy... you didn't tell me...
ARGY. I didn't know did I? I've never had one before. Thought I was going to die right there at the stage door.
THE AMBASSADOR. Would have sold a few albums I suppose (*off* ARGY'S *look*) *I'm nervous* – I've got 20,000 heads out front and my star act is...well...you don't look match-fit Argy.

A long beat.
THE AMBASSADOR *is trying to calculate the best thing to say.*
He is afraid that ARGY *will pull out of the gig.*

THE AMBASSADOR. Look, you ain't on your own kid. We have heroes in there to support you, *heroes*. We are talking veterans. There's not a one of them who wouldn't donate a kidney or a lung or a limb to you: you've got Yudi Thira on the drums. You've got Kasi on bass. You've got Brahma on lead guitar – the unconquerable Matt Vada is riding the keys like a golden chariot. You've got a pool of talent behind you. You are *supported*. You're not on your own out there, *is what I'm saying*.

We'll Live and Die in These Towns

ARGY *takes a deep sigh.*
He doesn't look convinced.

You ain't been right since you came home...this *crowd*...every other town, you go on stage and it's like the second coming... *miracles*...you come back here...it's like the magic drained out of your veins the minute you crossed the town border.

A beat.

What did you see Argy? When you looked through the stage door, at the heads, at the bodies – you was OK till I opened that door...what did you see?

ARGY *looks at* THE AMBASSADOR *long before answering.*

ARGY. I saw my father. I saw my mother, I saw my grandfather. I saw my uncles, my aunts, I saw my teachers. I saw my friends. I saw my brother, I saw my sister.

A beat.

When I looked out there I saw Jane.

THE AMBASSADOR *looks worried.*

My mouth is sand. I'm burning up.

ARGY *gets up.*

I can't do this. I can't go out there. I've got to get away. I'm forgetting myself.

Now it's the AMBASSADOR'S *turn to look pale.*

THE AMBASSADOR. Look, look you've had a funny turn *I understand that,* but let's not be in too much of a hurry to start cancelling things hey?

ARGY. I can't even hold my guitar. Look at me. I'm sweating like a rapist.

THE AMBASSADOR. You've still got a few hours yet...you'll be fine.

ARGY. These people, they all know me, they –

THE AMBASSADOR. Of course they know you – of course they do that's why they're here.

ARGY. Yea but they *know me* know me: they know I'm just some snotty council kid. They know I'm blagging it. I'll get slaughtered out there – and I'm supporting The Stones.

THE AMBASSADOR. That is fear talking! Don't you be listening to fear.

ARGY. I mean...The Stones!

THE AMBASSADOR. Fear is a soul-snatcher Argy –

ARGY. And the Stereophonics –

THE AMBASSADOR. *Dancing-in your mind* –

ARGY. The NME are in!

THE AMBASADOIR. She is trying to make you fall. DO NOT FALL.

ARGY (*his head has gone*). The NME are in!

THE AMBASSADOR. Listen. Argy, listen (ARGY *listens but he does not hear*). **Fear**...is a fat, slutty, mind-dancing fornicator of the truth!

ARGY. Oasis – I'm on the same stage as *the brothers.*

THE AMBASSADOR *grabs* ARGY'S *head urgently, trying to talk sense into him.*

THE AMBASSADOR. **Fear is a lie.** You panicked in there because you listened to her. She thinks she knows the answers, she thinks she knows what's good for you but fear is a delicious *incorrect* she'll convince you that a spill is a flood, that a flame is an inferno, she'll tell you that *here* is better than there and that *there* is better than here and that somewhere else, *anywhere else* is better than where you are right now. Not enough attention and she feels ignored, too much attention and she feels pressured – ***she lies!*** That doctor in there, what did he just tell you? You are perfectly healthy. You've got the lungs of a young elephant: you've got the constitution of a lion. You are not having a heart attack. You are not having a stroke...and the sky *chicken-licken*...is not about to fall in...if you believe fear – she will be on you, she'll be dancing (*taps* ARGY'S *head*) in here – and once you let her in, man, it'll be a 9-5 job trying to get her out again. Do not listen to fear Argy.

ARGY *steps away: Rabbit in the headlights.*
His mind captured by wild imaginings.

ARGY. I'm out of my depth.
THE AMBASSADOR (*exasperated*). You listened to fear.

THE AMBASSADOR *takes a step back, half resigned to the fact that* ARGY *is (at least temporarily) lost.*

ARGY. It's true. I'm not good enough.
THE AMBASSADOR. You shouldn't have listened.
ARGY. And if I go out there, in front of my friends, in front of my family, it's like I'm telling them 'I'm better that you'
THE AMBASSADOR. I warned you not to listen.

ARGY. It's like I'm pissing on them.

THE AMBASSADOR. Pissing on them you say!

ARGY. I step onto that stage, I'm gone. I'll never be able to get back.

THE AMBASSADOR. Get back to what?

ARGY. My old life will be dead.

THE AMBASSADOR. Hello! News flash. Your old life is already dead. You laid it to rest the minute you stepped away from the *minimum wage*, you killed it *dead* the moment picked up an instrument and threw out your song.

ARGY. I need to get away from here.

THE AMBASSSADOR. Ah that's interesting. When you did your forty-hour week with your name-badge and your, your, fucking guaranteed pension you said you needed to get away from *there too*.

ARGY (*holds his bursting head*). Look at me, I'm falling apart. I'd *rather* sell tellies on the high street again than feel like this.

THE AMBASSADOR (*irony*). Oh brilliant – every high street telly-salesman in the country wants to be a rock star, and the rock star wants to sell tellies on the high street.

ARGY (*panicking*). I don't want this, I can't -

THE AMBASSADOR (*Angry burst*). ARGY!! (ARGY *stops in his tracks*). This... (*the stadium*) this is what you've been building to. This is what you've been aiming for. How many shitty rooms have you played on your way to this arena? (ARGY *hesitates*) How many?

ARGY. Hundreds. I suppose.

THE AMBASSADOR. Thousands: pubs, working men's clubs, hotels, bars, christenings, weddings – *toilets!* Some of the venues you had to fight with drunks to get on the stage, some of them you had to fight with piss-heads to get *off* the stage – you left blood on the street kid.

ARGY. What's the use though, what's the point of having all this if I haven't got my family if I haven't got my friends?

THE AMBASSADOR. You can still have your family, it is not either or *either* – anyway I thought you said you wanted to escape the old life. Now you're saying you want to go back to it. Make your mind up.

ARGY. I don't want to run away from who I am.

THE AMBASSADOR. *Well* who the fuck *are* you?

That is a question
ARGY *thinks about it.*

ARGY. I don't know who I am. I only know that he ain't out there. That is not my stage.

THE AMBASSADOR. There are 40,000 eyes in that stadium all waiting to see you! Are you just going to walk away from that?

ARGY *stands, he paces, tries to rub the worry from his face: he looks like he might weep.*

ARGY. I don't know what's best for me anymore...*what is best for me?* Please tell me, I am dying here.

THE AMBASSADOR (compassionate). Lean in to the sharp edges kid *that's what's best for you.*

ARGY *looks confused and conflicted.*

Come.

THE AMBASSADOR *takes Argy's arm and gently leads him into –*
Lighting change.
*The **rehearsal room**.*

THE AMBASSADOR *approaches the band and speaks to them.*
We don't hear what he says.
The band play and THE AMBASSADOR *sings 'Pressure' as* ARGY *watches on.*

THE AMBASSADOR (*To* ARGY). Listen to the words Argy.

Pressure
https://www.youtube.com/watch?v=U6ccRsASPHw

THE AMBASSADOR.
Pressure, pressure, step into the pressure, don't
Let the pressure, let the pressure get you better
Keep a measure, measure on your pressure
Better check your pressure, watch out for the pressure
Take a little walk outside
It's easy, you know
Another thorn in your side
Working 9 to 5, she was a dancer
She's got it in her mind
She had the answer now
No, all she had was a show
To make your blood pump faster
Working 9 to 5, she was a dancer
She's got it in her mind
She had the answer now

We'll Live and Die in These Towns

No, all she had was a show
To make your blood pump faster
Pressure, pressure, step into the pressure, don't
Let the pressure, let the pressure get you better
Keep a measure, measure on the pressure
Better check your pressure, watch out for the pressure
Working 9 to 5, she was a dancer
She's got it in her mind
She had the answer now
No, all she had was a show
To make your blood pump faster
Working 9 to 5, she was a dancer
She's got it in her mind
She had the answer now
No, all she had was a show
To make your blood pump faster

The song finishes.

THE AMBASSADOR (To ARGY). Go out there. Take your stage. You'll be fine. I promise you, the song will not let you down.

ARGY. I can't. I can't I can't *I've already lost people*, on the way; *real people*.

THE AMBASSADOR. Argy. The song is the *only* thing that is real. You can lose everything else on this spinning planet, and eventually you will, we all will, but you can't lose the song: it is indestructible. It is eternal. It is immutable – we are all going to live and die in these shitty towns, in these stinking, rotting bodies, but the song, who can kill the song? If you drop dead on that stage right now it'll pick up another body like that (clicks his fingers) and some other flag-bearer will carry it. If you fade away, it'll slide you off like an old coat: *the song will prevail.*

ARGY. Things used to be simpler.

THE AMBASSADOR *shakes his head, exasperated.*
He takes a CD from his inside pocket.
He points angrily to one of the songs listed on the back cover.

THE AMBASSADOR. Sing it. Remind yourself of how simple things *really* used to be.

ARGY *looks at the song. He shakes his head.*

Consider it a warm up. Think of it as a rehearsal.
ARGY. I don't want to sing any more.
THE AMBASSADOR. You don't want to sing... the people have paid! I've paid. Forty years in the desert building a stage for you.

THE AMBASSADOR *thrusts the guitar into* ARGY'S *chest.*
ARGY *does not take it.*

(*Angry*) no? All right then. If you won't sing one for me, I'll sing one for you shall I bearing in mind I can't sing to save my own life. (*To the band*) Boys.

THE AMBASSADOR *sings 'Had Enough'.*

Had Enough
https://www.youtube.com/watch?v=iPTBu9hD57U

We'll Live and Die in These Towns

THE AMBASSADOR.
Give me a good enough reason
Why I should not cut you down
You've been taking too much
Ever since you started hanging round this crowd
And I've had enough, had enough
Yes, you let me down, let me down, now now now
I'm giving up, giving up
Yes, I'll see you round, see you round, now now now
Hey, hey
What's the matter with your face, face?
When you had it your way, way
Won't you give me some time to understand your mind
Oooo it's alright
Oooo it's alright
Let me say what I want
Don't you know it was on the tip of my tongue
If you opened your eyes
Took a look outside
You would see you're wrong
And I've had enough, had enough
Yes, you let me down, let me down, now now now
I'm giving up, giving up
Yes, I'll see you round, see you round, see you round, now, now now
Hey, hey
What's the matter with your face, face
When you had it your way, way
Won't you give me some time to understand your mind
Oooo it's alright
Oooo it's alright
Had enough, had enough

Had enough, had enough
Had enough, had enough, let me down
Had enough had enough, see you around
Had enough had enough, let me down
Had enough, had enough, I'll see you around
Hey, hey
What's the matter with your face, face?
When you had it your way, way
Won't you give me some time to understand your mind

The song ends
THE AMBASSADOR *thrusts the guitar at* ARGY *again.*

THE AMBASSADOR. Now you! Sing. Like you did when you walked into my office ten years ago. A spotty, spunky, snot dribble of a kid – 21 years old – you nearly ripped the plaster off my ceiling with your arrogance.

ARGY *hesitates.*

You dishonour yourself Argy. You dishonour me. You dishonour the boys. You dishonour the kids out there that have paid to see you. This is a man's game, and this *cowardly* behaviour is not....*manly*.

This triggers a response from ARGY: *angry now, he snatches the guitar from the Ambassador and belts out Away From Here.*

Away From Here
https://www.youtube.com/watch?v=7ZCVds_Q3WE

We'll Live and Die in These Towns

I'm so sick, sick, sick and tired
Of working just to be retired
I don't want to get that far
I don't want your company car
Promotions aint my thing
Name badges are not interesting
It's much easier for me see
To stay at home with Richard and Judy
Awayaway oh oh oh away from here...
Awayaway oh oh oh away from here
Awayaway oh oh oh away from here
Awayaway oh oh oh away from here
I'm fed up of early mornings
Wake up calls are getting boring round here
Feet dragging on the pavement
The same people with the same arrangement
Irony can be quite funny
You making other people money
My working day has just begun
Its not exactly what I would call fun
I want to wake up in the afternoon
With daytime tv and my favourite tune
Cos it is much easier for me see
To stay at home with Richard and Judy
Awayaway oh oh oh away from here.....
Away away away away from
Saturday is your only highlight
When you go out and live the highlife
Meeting up with other people
Your interaction with the weak and feeble
At least when all is said and done
You wouldn't be the only one

To be a slave to the modern wage
Your crappy weekend is your only escape
I want to wake up in the afternoon
With daytime tv and my favourite tune
Cos it is much easier for me
To stay at home with Richard and Judy
Awayaway oh oh oh away from here.....
Away away away away from here

The song ends.

THE AMBASSADOR (*impressed*). When you walked into my office *desperate* to be signed you weren't just going to make it big, you was going to take your stage and show everyone else how it was done – it was like scripture to you. Somewhere between my office and that stage door you've forgotten your gospel.

ARGY'S *head drops.*
He still looks depressed and dissonant.

ARGY. What is the point? What is the point of *anything*?
THE AMBASSADOR. Every time *one...very...brave* person breaks the *dance of fear* and sings his own unique song **everyone** benefits. Every time one frightened person turns away from the song, **everyone** suffers. You understand? Everyone.

THE AMBASSADOR *takes the CD case out again.*
He removes the sleeve with the lyrics.
He hands them to ARGY.

Read.

ARGY *reads the lyrics to one of his songs.*

You're not alone.
ARGY *nods.*

ARGY. I know.
THE AMBASSADOR. No, you Doris. The song: 'You're Not Alone.' Read the lines Argy (ARGY *hesitates*). Indulge me.

The AMBASSADOR *surreptitiously signals the band to play. The band quietly plays the first chords of* 'You're Not Alone'.

https://www.youtube.com/watch?v=mpzOejM5CrU

ARGY (*reads/gently sings the lyrics*). Don't let the sun go down on our empire...it's too much to waste. (THE AMBASSADOR *encourages him to read more*). And don't let the walls come down round our empire...
THE AMBASSADOR (*Sings gently*). It's too much to wave goodbye... we've been working for a long time...we've been fighting for a way...

The band breaks fully into the song.
ARGY *raises his hand in the air, indicating that the band stop playing.*
The band stops.

ARGY. I want to go home.

THE AMBASSADOR *looks sad and resigned. He nods knowingly.*

I need to go home.

THE AMBASSADOR. I know.
ARGY. I want to see my brother. I want to see my sister. (A beat) I want to see Jane. (Beat) It's her birthday today.

THE AMBASSADOR *looks at the floor in despair; he knows what comes next.*

I didn't send her a card.

THE AMBASSADOR *nods knowingly.*

And now I'm here. The dream. And it don't stack up. The dream is not delivering.
THE AMBASSADOR. *You're* not delivering Argy, and you're blaming it on something else, anything else. That's how it really stacks up. (Off ARGY'S offended reaction) You're stuck in a forest of delusion kid. I'm just trying to drag you out.

ARGY *looks perplexed.*
THE AMBASSADOR *comes to a decision.*

Look. I tell you what. (*Points to exit door*) See that door. That's the past. Take a little walk. Drag your boot-heels along yesterday's pavements. Go and see your sister. Go and see your brother, call Jesus down from the heavens if you think it'll help – and drop in on Jane, why not. If you can find your old life *back there*, stay, by all means, go back to the local bars singing your song where you feel safe, you won't be the first and you won't be the last. See that door (*re: the stage door*). That is the future, the gate-less gate, behind it is the milk-and-honey – if you *really* want to sing your song (*looks at his watch*) you're due on stage in four hours.

ARGY *looks at both doors: he is torn.*

You ever read The Bhagavad-Gita? (ARGY *shakes his head*) no, nor have I, but I was handed a leaflet once by a *follower* on Oxford Street – Genie trouser, Nike trainers, banging a tambourine off his head – it had some nice words on the front (*quotes*): '*Whatever actions a great man performs, common men follow. And whatever standards he sets by exemplary acts, all the world pursues*'.

THE AMBASSADOR *walks out.*
ARGY *is alone.*
He looks around him, trying to make a decision.
ARGY *picks up his guitar and exits.*
We hear the opening bars of 'It's Not OK.'
A lighting change.

It's Not OK
https://www.youtube.com/watch?v=o03awtSlbkY

BUSKER (*off*)
Stop living your life for the alarm
that wakes you up every day at eight
leave your Peugeot on the forecourt
it's all too much for you to take

A lighting change.
ARGY is *walking along a high street.*

Geoff Thompson

ARGY *walks past (and stops to look at)* **a shitty supermarket, a petrol station** *with* 'SOLD OUT' *on the pumps.*
An old, weathered BUSKER *is sat in a shop doorway.*
He is next to an electrical shop, with loads of TV's for sale in the window.
BUSKER *is wrapped under three coats, a scarf and a woolly hat.*
He is playing a guitar.
He is surrounded by all his worldly possessions:
A battered guitar case, a dirty rucksack, a muddy quilt **and a stuffed, mangy dog, on wheels.**

BUSKER *is singing 'It's Not OK.'*

BUSKER
your girlfriend don't love you but still she slaves
to make a home for you to stay
the people above you they keep you held down
the boys, the boys you'd love to make
leaning on your fence when you told me
you were gonna make lots of money
be a princess, diamonds and cigarettes
rolling out the carpet to regrets
now you're not so young it's too easy
to be a dreamer, wake up and be free
your clock is ticking fast friend, believe me
you only get one chance, can you hear me

ARGY *stops listens to* BUSKER.

BUSKER
it's not OK to be this way
it's not OK to be a slave

We'll Live and Die in These Towns

BUSKER *sees* ARGY'S *guitar and nods to him: 'join in.'*
BUSKER *clearly doesn't recognise* ARGY.
ARGY *sings.*
BUSKER *plays guitar.*

ARGY
stop living your life for a man in a tie
he's just a fool the same as you
his daughter don't love him but still he slaves
to make a way for her to choose
her teenage dreams are here today
but in the morning they'll be gone
washed away by the minimum wage
the same, the same as everyone.

BUSKER
leaning on your fence when you told me
you were gonna make lots of money
be a princess, diamonds and cigarettes
rolling out the carpet to regrets
now you're not so young it's too easy
to be a dreamer, wake up and be free
your clock is ticking fast friend, believe me
you only get one chance, can you hear me

BUSKER/ARGY
it's not OK to be this way
it's not OK to be a slave

ARGY
leaning on your fence when you told me
you were gonna make lots of money

be a princess, diamonds and cigarettes
rolling out the carpet to regrets
now you're not so young it's too easy
to be a dreamer, wake up and be free
your clock is ticking fast friend, believe me
you only get one chance, can you hear me

BUSKER/ARGY
it's not OK to be this way
not OK to be this way
not OK to be this way
not OK to be a slave
to be a slave
to be a slave

The song ends.
ARGY *drops a twenty-pound note in the* BUSKER'S *guitar case and walks away.*
The BUSKER *looks shocked: twenty quid!*

BUSKER (*after him*). Hey, you ain't bad.

ARGY *stops.*

ARGY. Thanks.
BUSKER. I reckon you could probably make a living at it... you know, if you put in a bit more practice.

ARGY *smiles at the irony.*

Do you know any more?

ARGY. I've got to be somewhere.
BUSKER. Do you know 'This Song?'
ARGY. I'm meeting someone.
BUSKER. Don't you want to play?

ARGY *hesitates.*

I'll share the take.

ARGY *smiles.*

ARGY. Another time maybe.

ARGY *walks.*

BUSKER. Might not be another time brother.

A lighting change.
Snow starts to fall gently.
ARGY *pulls up his hood and turns his collar against the cold.*
He stops at a table outside a **rough cafe.**
He sits and takes in his surroundings.
He strums a tune (the opening bars of '40 Days and 40 Nights')
He sings the first lines, as though he has just written them.
People walk past as he sings.
One or two drop coins in his case

40 Days and 40 Nights
https://www.youtube.com/watch?v=6iegJIU4IH0

ARGY
I took a walk to the supermarket

It was so cold
I couldn't get back home
Through all the snow
Took A Vacation To The Petrol Station.
They Were Sold Out
I couldn't Get Back Home
They Didn't Want To Know.

Someone shouts: 'get a fucking job.'

It jars ARGY.
He stops singing and puts his guitar away.
He gets up and walks.
A lighting change.
ARGY *stands at the door of a terraced house.*
He nervously lifts his hand to knock.
He hesitates.
As he makes to knock again the door opens.
A heavy-set girl (HIPS) *appears in the doorway.*
She is grumpy and unwelcoming.

ARGY. Hi…I thought I'd just pop by, see how he is
HIPS. He's sleeping.

A beat.

ARGY. How is he?
HIPS. He's dying, that's how he is. My husband has cancer, he has heart failure. He's chronic. And…he's sleeping. We weren't expecting company. I thought you was on a stage somewhere today, making lots of money.

ARGY. I was just. I was passing so. I nipped out and I thought. I'm supposed to be on stage in *(looks at his watch)* three and a half hours. Twenty thousand people.
HIPS. It's alright for some. Anyway, as I said, he's sleeping.
BILL *(off)*. Who's at the door?

HIPS *gives* ARGY *a stare: 'now you've woken him'.*

HIPS (to BILL). It's no one. You're sleeping. *(To* ARGY*)* He's asleep.

ARGY *looks past her to the door;* BILL *is patently awake*

I'll tell him you called.

ARGY *makes to walk away.*
BILL *appears behind* HIPS.

BILL. Is that my brother, is that you Argy?
ARGY. I was just passing.

BILL *hugs* ARGY *heartily.*

BILL. Well don't *just* pass, *just* stop, *just* come in, you're my brother, come in come in *ten times come in* (to HIPS). Why didn't you send him in you Doris, he's my brother?
HIPS. Because you're asleep
BILL. Do I look like I'm asleep?
HIPS. The place is upside-down.
BILL. The place is a palace.
HIPS. I haven't hoovered.
BILL. He's my brother. He's not the health inspector.

HIPS *turns moodily and disappears into the black.*

(To ARGY*).* Argy. Enter the Ashram.

Lights fully up.
We are in BILL'S *front room.*
Two armchairs face each other on a threadbare carpet.
BILL *lowers himself painfully into one of the armchairs.*
He is clearly suffering.
ARGY *sits opposite him.*

HIPS *(off)*. Do you want food?
BILL. No I do not want food. (*Pause*) Yes, all right then – a *snacket*. (*Pause*) No. Not yet. After. *(*To ARGY*)* she's a good girl but I think she's trying to feed me to my grave *(pats his belly)*. There are worse ways to go I suppose.

ARGY *looks at* BILL, *he's huge.*

(Re. *his weight*) I know I know, but it's all I've got left. They took my cigarettes off me didn't they, *the doctors*, they took my beer – you know how I like a beer – they ain't having my food as well. Do *you* want something to eat? (ARGY *shakes his head)* I can get her to rustle something up for us, no problem – she can murder us both at the same time.

BILL *laughs at his own joke.*

Anyway. You. My little brother. It's been a while
ARGY. I know, I'm sorry. I've –
BILL. Hey! I'm as bad. I could call *you*, but I don't. So why the err *(visit)?*

ARGY. I was just passing.
BILL. You're never just passing; my abode is in the Siberian outskirts of Coventry *no one is ever just passing*.
ARGY. I've been thinking about you. Lately. Today. I wanted to see you.

An uncomfortable pause.

BILL. I hear you on the radio.

ARGY *nods*.

You sing a *rare* song.

ARGY *smiles his thanks*.

Plenty of money? Females? *Of course*. Women love a man with a song. Christ you see the skirt hanging off the arm of those *ugly* rock stars – if they were working in the call centre, or on the shop floor, they wouldn't get a look in, we couldn't get within a mile of the office secretary at our place, two O levels and a college course in accounting and suddenly they're above the man with oil on his hands.
ARGY. It's not really about the money for me Bill or the skirt.
BILL. No, I know that; it's about the poetry. But the money and the skirt, you're not going to say no are you?
ARGY. Are you still writing?

BILL *shakes his head*.

BILL. You're a hard act to follow.
ARGY. I always thought I was following you.

BILL. There's no market for verse. No one wants to buy a poem anymore, not that I ever sold one (*indicates* HIPS) she always reminds me of that.

ARGY. You used to love the words. You always had a pen in your hand.

BILL (*mimics pen in fingers*). Aaron's rod *my Parker Pen* – spilling with inky-manna – I used to weave magic with that nib, I could turn a staff into a snake and back again – it had its own life, it was biblical.

ARGY. I remember when you worked nights in the hospital –

BILL. Inspiring stuff pushing dead bodies back and forward to the morgue. People – listen to this Argy, people going from birth to death within a 5-mile radius, what you think about that –- and with every *cadaver* you shift you think *this is one departure closer to my own:* one day it'll be me lying stiff on that trolley off to the knacker's yard. You're delivering the dead from the ward to the morgue thinking 'these bodies are the bodies of people that have never left this town'...except for the holiday fortnight once a year when every worker-ant leaves the minimum wage *en-mass* for two weeks of sand-and-sea between their toes on a Skegness beach – how fucking despairing is that.

ARGY. Yeah but remember you told me, you used to sit on the hospital roof at midnight – when all the bosses had gone home – you'd sit there with your pen and pad looking out onto the town.

BILL. I did.

ARGY. You said the streets spread out in front of you like an exotic creature, like it was alive.

BILL (*smiles*). Looked like the breathing embers of last night's bonfire, glowing and hissing and spitting red when you poked it with a stick.

ARGY. You said you could see the cathedral, you said you could see the three spires, the football ground, the sky-blues.
BILL. Cinderella – she comes alive at midnight, this town.
ARGY (*quotes a poem*). 'An industrious town is this, prone to layoffs and strikes, always something amiss, likes and dislikes alike.'
BILL. 'The three spired city that inspired pity on the cap with the button, the industrious glutton.'
ARGY. *Your* words Bill.

BILL *smiles remembering his own verse.*
BILL *removes* ARGIE'S *flat-cap and admires it.*
The cap has seven neatly sewn panels.

BILL. The cap with the button. *Coventry* cap. Did you know that?
ARGY. I think you told me once, when I was a kid.
BILL. Usually made from green or brown tweed with a stiffened peak. When this city was still a town, it had seven gates, they all led into the centre. (*Shows on the cap*) Each of the seven panels represents one of those gates, and the button in the centre...always had a farthing on it.

BILL *puts the cap back on* ARGY'S *head.*

ARGY. I loved reading your poems.
BILL. I loved writing my poems.
ARGY. Why did you stop?
BILL. Why did I stop? Now then, there's a question. (He thinks) At first it was just about the words. Words were my testament and I had a blind faith in every verse. Faith Argy, faith that offered no guarantees other than one – *when*

you serve the poem the service itself is the highest reward because it delivers the *milk and honey*. I used to exist on a cloud of pure faith, just thinking about the word, no desire for paper *(indicates money)*, no claims of ownership, no fight, no lethargy, my bliss came through the wordage and the rhythm on the page. Ahhhh the seas I could part with the nib of my pen. But then...I *did* start thinking about the paper – I *wanted* guarantees: who's going to pay me, my rent ain't going to find itself, other people are getting all the accolades, why not me? Then it was not about faith anymore and it was not about the word, it was about lust... the $, the £, the golden Calf...and lust is never sated, that is one thing I do know, it burns like fire...then of course when the paper did not appear ***anger!*** Delusion quickly followed, then bewilderment. Suddenly...a drought...my pen is parched. All I'm left with is concrete arteries and an empty page.

A beat.

My poem is here now Argy *(pats his big belly)* and here, *(touches his heart)* and here *(touches his groin):* Pain is my poetry, pain...and it alights at every hour even though I do not invite it.

ARGY *looks sad at hearing this.*

The muse...she stopped calling. Well, maybe she did call once or twice and maybe I just didn't answer. You can only turn her away so many times before she stops visiting altogether. I made an agreement see; *you bring me the words and I'll give them a page*. I didn't keep my covenant. So now I'm blocked, now I'm tangled. The only *easy* I get these days is from the food. And the sleep when I can snaffle an hour.

A beat.

Anyway, you didn't come here to hear about by twisted entrails and blocked arteries – what ails you? You are troubled I can see.
ARGY. I'm all right.
BILL. You look like you lost something. Did you lose something?

ARGY *sighs but does not answer.*

One thing I learned from pushing dead bodies around Arg: most of them go to their grave with their best song still in them, and that's a waste.

ARGY *nods.*
He understands.

Anyone that follows the song, but then loses the song, is lost to the past *and* the future. I'm living proof of that maxim.
ARGY. Can I do anything for *you* Bill? Do you need anything? Do you need money?
BILL. I don't need money I don't want money (*Re. his mangled body*) it won't help, not even if you give me all the money in the world. (BILL *leans forward with an urgent desire*) I'll tell you what I do need though Arg; I'll tell you what I would like, if you'll oblige me.

ARGY *nods 'anything'*
BILL'S *eyes fall on* ARGY's *guitar.*

A song for your brother. A private audience.

ARGY *smiles.*
He seems delighted that he can do this one small thing for BILL.
He takes out his guitar.

ARGY. What do you want me to sing?
BILL. The one about the old days, when we sat in that smoky club and dreamed of being somewhere else, somewhere better.

ARGY *strums the opening chords of 'We'll Live and Die In These Towns.'*
BILL *smiles, sinks back into his chair and closes his eyes: bliss.*
ARGY *sings 'We'll Live and Die In These Towns.'*
(Note: BILL joins in the song at certain points).

We'll Live and Die in These Towns
https://www.youtube.com/watch?v=7miErQzz4Y8

ARGY
You spend your time in smoky rooms
Where haggled old women
With cheap perfume say
It never happens for people
Like us you know
Well nothing ever happened on its own
And well the toilets smell of desperation
The streets all echo of aggravation
and you wonder.
Why you can't get no sleep.
When you've got nothing to do,

We'll Live and Die in These Towns

And you've had nothing to eat.
Your life's slipping
And sliding right out of view
And there's absolutely nothing
That you can do well

We'll live and die,
We'll live and die in these towns
Don't let it drag you down
Don't let it drag you down now
We'll live and die,
We'll live and die in these towns
Don't let it drag you down
Don't let it drag you down now
Dirty dishes from a TV meal
That went cold from the wind
Through a smashed up window
You can't go out if anybody calls ya
Cos you can't have a bath
When there's no hot water
And your friends are out
On the town again.
And you ask yourself if it will ever end
And it's all too much for your head to take.
Just a matter of time
Before you break, well
We'll live and die
We'll live and die in these towns
Don't let it drag you down
Don't let it drag you down now
We'll live and die,
We'll live and die in these towns

Don't let it drag you down
Don't let it drag you down now

Now...
Now...

We'll live and die,
We'll live and die in these towns
Don't let it drag you down
Don't let it drag you down now
We'll live and die,
We'll live and die in these towns
Don't let it drag you down
Don't let it drag you down now

The song ends.
BILL *has tears running down his face.*

BILL. Leaking (*wipes his tears*). I think you may have re-ignited the embers. I might get the Parker back out later – I can feel the muse calling again – perhaps she hasn't abandoned me after all.

The word 'abandon' stirs something deep in ARGY.
We see it on his face.
BILL *sees it too, and he leans forward, grabs* ARGY'S *hands lovingly.*

We used to talk me and you...into the night. Do you remember?
ARGY. I loved it.
BILL. In the club, over a pint.

ARGY (*nods effusively*).

BILL. We were going to make it.

Some sadness from BILL, *perhaps that he did not make it.*

One day we were really going to make it...it's what kept me alive.
ARGY. You was going to write the poetry and plays and scripts – you sent them off to the BBC.
BILL. (*Re. HIPS*) She typed them out for me...typed her fingers red-raw. A neatly bound manuscript inserted into a manila envelope, pushed into the mouth of a post box. I can still *feel* it now – my dreams on the wings of two first class stamps.
ARGY (*Laughs*). Then weeks of waiting for a reply.
BILL. Months sometimes, but ahhhh the hope – in the waiting... there was hope.
ARGY. Then it comes back, your envelope.
BILL. BBC stamped all over the front – you always knew if it was a rebuttal if it came back in a large envelope.
ARGY. That meant they'd sent your script back.
BILL. Usually unread.
ARGY. You can tell can't you?
BILL. Pages still pristine, clearly untouched.
ARGY. 'Dear Sir, thank you for your submission.'
BILL. Insults the intelligence Argy – didn't even have the decency to fake a fresh thumb-print on the corner of the page – 'We are very sorry but on this occasion...'
ARGY. I had hundreds like that, more.
BILL. Crushing. But you sit down again, and you write again –
ARGY. And you send it out again.
BILL. Of course you do – then another loooong wait.

ARGY. The idea of selling a piece of work …it was like a lottery win to people like us, wasn't it.
BILL. It tempers you *the rejection*.

ARGY *nods, this resonates.*

Then people start to lose their belief in you. I suppose that's a part of it. 'When you going to get a real job?'
ARGY. 'How you gonna feed your family?'
BILL. 'Your poems ain't going to pay for the electric?'
ARGY. 'There's no food in the fridge, and you're sat on your arse writing songs.'
BILL. 'We won't get a mortgage if you ain't got a regular wage.'
ARGY. 'But you've *got* to keep your job. It's safe – '
BILL. 'It's a job for life.' (*Laughs*) job for life – that's what I was bloody worried about.
ARGY. 'Jobs like this don't grow on trees.'
BILL. Thank fuck for that!

Both laugh.

ARGY. Lashes ain't it Bill…when people stop believing in you.
BILL. Eventually you stop believing in yourself. That hurts more.

ARGY *nods, he knows.*

(*Emotional*). It is *agony*… (*beat*) sitting down, writing lines that no one is ever going to read. (*Laughs ironically*) and it is **pure agony** thinking *one day, people **might** read them and think 'this is bloody shit!'* (*Laughs*) can't (*coughing*) can't win (*laugh/cough*). What if they fucking hate my poems?

BILL *goes into a laugh-and-cough frenzy.*
ARGY *stands and rubs* BILL'S *back.*
BILL *waves him off 'I'm OK.'*
ARGY *watches his brother suffer, and it is excruciating.*
BILL *eventually calms.*

The dilemma of an artist hey Argy. (*Pause*) In the end – and this is the bit when you know you're lost – in the end you even start to doubt the investment of two first class stamps and a manila envelope.

The atmosphere has become a little melancholy.

You broke through. That's something.
ARGY (*guilt*). What about the ones that don't break through?
BILL. The ones that do...*they* speak for the ones that don't. And that's a big job right there. Large job. Weighty. I'm glad it was you that made it out, not me, (*off* ARGY'S *confusion*). I'm like the masses Arg, I like the idea of my *god-like-possibilities*, but I'm not so keen on the *god-like-responsibilities* that come with it – *I wouldn't cope*. I can't handle normal life: I'd collapse completely if you put the weight of success on me

A long beat.

ARGY. I feel like I'm leaving everyone behind, Bill.

BILL *smiles sadly; suddenly he understands why* ARGY *is here.*

BILL (*compassion/understanding*). Argy!!!!!

BILL *sings a few lines from* ARGY'S *songs*:

(*Sings gently*). 'Half the kids that you grew up with were pushing prams by the time they were just sixteen.' That line, it glows like a shining lamp. You're taking us with you, in the words. We're there...in the song. (*Sings*) 'All the boys and all their toys couldn't see the signs as we scorched out eyes with nicotine'...that is the *butter and fire* of my life. (*Sings*) 'If love is a drug, then where is the cure, for the girl who used to talk to you about her dreams' (*looks at* ARGY, *with some poignancy*). Shell. That's our Shelly, our kid (*sings*) 'leaning on your fence when you told me, you were gonna make lots of money, be a princess, diamonds and cigarettes, rolling out the carpet for regrets...' 'And the grownups said, listen to your head, but our hearts were crying out for heroes on TV screens.' That's me, that's our dad, that's our mum (*sings*) 'this song, this song is about you, this song is about you.' You never left anyone, you Doris.

In the background we hear the haunting brass opening of 'This Song.'

ARGY. Not everyone thinks that Bill.

BILL *muses on this for a moment.*
He can see that ARGY *is perplexed.*

BILL. When did you ever care about what *anyone* else thought? Nothing worth a toss was ever created by a committee, you know that. The moment you care about what other people think, you're back in your cell, in the dark, *a good boy doing as you're told,* chained to the mores. You care about what other people think Argy, you become their prisoner.

ARGY. 'An artist should never be a member of anyone's club'... you always told me that.

BILL. Never work for money, never work for approval – money and approval are the death-knell of creativity. The song withers under the weight of expectation – expectation is a *thorny* crown.

BILL stretches his neck and arms.
He sighs deeply as though suddenly exhausted.

Ohhhhh. I'm tired now Argy. I might need to close my eyes.

ARGY nods.

BILL closes his eyes.

I'm tired. Just going to close my eyes for a second, you don't mind do you? You won't think bad of me will you?

BILL falls asleep on the chair.
HIPS appears from behind BILL'S chair.

HIPS *(unkind/to* ARGY*)*. He's asleep. He doesn't want to be awoken.

ARGY makes to leave but then stops.
He goes back to BILL'S chair.
ARGY removes his Coventry cap.
He places it gently on BILL'S head.
He leans in and kisses BILL.

He holds the kiss long.
It is undeniably full of love.
HIPS *sees this and something moves in her.*
ARGY *leaves.*
As though she's heard the background music for 'This Song,'
HIPS *gently sings the chorus.*
ARGY *stops and listens.*

This Song (chorus)
https://www.youtube.com/watch?v=ZM7n6cXIdCU

HIPS
Changes in your mind,
Changes in your life,
Changes in the times,
And the reason you can't sleep at night,
Changes in your mind,
Changes in your life,
Changes in the times,
And the reason you gave up the fight.
Now this song is about you,
Now this song is about...

She stops singing

I had my dreams.

HIPS *looks at* BILL *in the chair asleep.*

My dreams were interrupted.

ARGY *nods, sadly.*

We'll Live and Die in These Towns

Your brother is *asleep* in that chair. Do you understand? (ARGY *nods*) Your brother will die in that chair.

ARGY'S *head slumps.*

Don't *you* be falling asleep?

A lighting change.

We break fully into 'This Song.'

This Song
https://www.youtube.com/watch?v=ZM7n6cXIdCU

BUSKER
Half the kids that you grew up with
Were pushing prams by the time that they were just sixteen
If love is a drug then where is the cure
For the girl who used to talk to you about her dream

ARGY
And all the boys with all their toys
Couldn't see the signs as we scorched out eyes with nicotine
And the grown-ups said listen to your heads
But our hearts were crying out for heroes on TV screens

ARGY/BUSKER
Now this song is about you
Now this song is about…

HIPS
Changes in your mind

Geoff Thompson

Changes in your lives
Changes in the times
And the reason you can't sleep at night
Changes in your mind
Changes in your lives
Changes in the times
And the reason you gave up the fight

ARGY
Half the kids that aren't pushing prams
Are now pushing pills to boys and girls who are half their age
And the pubs and clubs are full of drunks
Who don't remember the day they were born or even remember their names
An old man sings a tune he knew but he's drowned out by a fight next to a fruit machine
And all of this, our hearts, our nation
Total lack of civilization
Will it ever be the same?

ARGY/BUSKER
Now this song is about you
Now this song is about…

HIPS (possibly with ARGY and BUSKER)
Changes in your mind
Changes in your lives
Changes in the times
And the reason you won't sleep tonight
Changes in your mind
Changes in our lives
Changes in the times

We'll Live and Die in These Towns

And the reason we gave up the fight

As the song nears its end, ARGY *suddenly appears on the screen behind them.*
He is in a promo video for his Throne Room gig.
Both ARGY *and* BUSKER *stop and watch the screen.*
BUSKER *does a double-take.*
It suddenly dawns on him who ARGY *really is.*

BUSKER. That you? On the telly.
ARGY (*dissonant*). I used to sell tellies...now I'm on telly.

BUSKER *strums cords from 'this song' on his guitar.*

BUSKER. How is it then? Life. On a big screen.
ARGY. Different.
BUSKER. Good different or bad different?
ARGY. You should go and see for yourself.

BUSKER *smiles sadly, he grabs the dog's lead, and pulls the (stuffed) dog towards him, on its wheels.*

BUSKER. I would but. I've got my dog ain't I? I couldn't leave my dog.

ARGY *nods, this speaks to him.*

Anyway I ain't ready yet. I need more time, I need more practice.

The irony of BUSKERS *words are not lost on* ARGY.
ARGY *walks away.*

BUSKER *sings the chorus of 'This Song.'*
He sings it slow.
He sings it with melancholy.

BUSKER
Now this song…is about, is about, is about you (x8)

LIGHTS OUT.

INTERVAL.

PART 2

Lights up.
We are outside the paint-flaking front doors of 'The Three Spires' working men's club.
ARGY *walks to the front door.*
He takes in the building like he is looking at an old friend.

SHELLY *(off)*. Ohhh....my famous brother.

ARGY *turns and sees* SHELLY.
It is his drunken sister.
She staggers towards him.
She has a bottle of cider in her coat pocket.
She takes a slug, and then puts it back.
His face drops. His heart sinks.
SHELLY *stands in front of him.*
She looks him up and down arrogantly.
She surveys his clothing like she is doing a value assessment.
She examines the quality of his jacket, by feeling the lapel.

Pricey...pay my rent for a month that.

He makes to take his jacket off.

ARGY. Do you want it Shell? You can have it.

She dismisses his gesture.

SHELLY. Thought you'd be too good for this place now.

ARGY *looks sad.*

This was good enough for our mum.

ARGY *drops his head*

They all know you know. In there (*the club*) they're not thick. I'm not thick: although apparently, I'm the one in the family with a drink problem (*she slugs from the cider bottle/puts it back in her pocket*). They know you write about them.
ARGY. I write about what I know bab, I just –
SHELLY (*emotional*). This place was good enough for *our* dad.
ARGY. I love this place, you know that, I love these people –
SHELLY (*interrupts on 'people'*). That why you write such *shit* about them then? (*A beat/with spite*) This place was good enough for Jane!

Boom! This hits ARGY *like a hammer.*

ARGY. I left her. I know.
SHELLY. You abandoned her, you abandoned us all.

ARGY *is destroyed by this*

She knew. She knew all about you. She knew all about the girls, all the other girls –
ARGY. That wasn't just me she –
SHELLY. Everyone knew –
ARGY. Jane sacked *me*, Jane said –
SHELLY (*sarcastic*). Jane said! Jane said 'I think we should have a little break' that's what Jane said, 'I think a little break will do us both good, see how we feel about each

other' she was testing you, y' donkey. Testing! It's what girls do. You know she never meant it, she thought you'd fall over yourself to fight for her –
ARGY. I couldn't be what she wanted me to be Shell...she used to love my song; she used to write all my lyrics out for me...then suddenly she hated my words, wouldn't even look at them –
SHELLY. Yea, well it must be hard writing out words and reading *every – intimate – detail* about your own life on a page – some things are meant to be private you know!

ARGY *looks battered.*

ARGY. I just. I write about what I see Shell, I –
SHELLY. Yea, well maybe you should stop writing about what you see: maybe what *you* see is what other people ***don't*** want to see, you ever thought about that.

ARGY *is silent.*

No, course not, 'cus all you think about is yourself.
ARGY. I wanted her to come with me, I didn't want to do this on my own, I begged her to come with me –
SHELLY (*interrupts on 'me'*). Come with you and do what? Carry your bags? Make you cups of tea? Sit in a hotel room looking at the wallpaper all day while you *swan it* on the telly and the radio and in your posh magazines –
ARGY. That's not kind Shell –
SHELLY. Doesn't have to be kind does it. It just has to be true.

SHELLY *slugs from the cider bottle.*
ARGY *watches sadly.*

(*Off* ARGY'S *reaction*). Jane's mum hates your bones did you know that. (*Re. club*) and *they* all hate you – in there. Writing about them – the only reason I don't hate you is because we share blood. (*Beat*) You didn't even bother changing their names did you? Then you fucked off, once you got what you wanted, once you'd fleeced us – that why you're back, you need more stories do you, come back to pick on the bones? They're our stories that you stole. Ours! (*Beat*) It's her birthday today you know. Jane. (*Accusation*) you didn't get her a card, did you.

ARGY *opens his mouth to answer.*
Nothing comes out but silence and guilt.
He is saved further shame by:
The club doors burst open.
A group of three 'oiled' people spill from the club.
MEGAN, SAMMY and DANNY.
They are laughing and joking and in high spirits.
MEGAN *is the first to recognise* ARGY.

MEGAN. Oh mate, it's Argy – look it's him. (*She spots* SHELLY) Hey up Shell – you didn't tell me your brother was home mate (SHELLY *shrugs*) (*To* ARGY) tell them, that song you wrote, that's about me ain't it mate – ah mate, I'm Megan – that's about us ain't it – (*points to her friends*) Danny, Sammy, Megan? They don't believe me, tell him mate, tell them it's true.

ARGY *nods in the affirmative.*
They all cheer uproariously; their claim to fame.

SAMMY. You should pay us royalties man (*laughs*).

DANNY (*sings*). Danny was a bad boy. He liked to kick and scream and shout.

They all laugh.
SHELLY *looks pissed that* ARGY *is getting so much attention.*

MEGAN. Seriously though mate, really honoured, really honoured mate that you wrote about me, it's like, oh mate, it ain't every day that some *rock dude* writes a song about you.

MEGAN *hugs* ARGY, *takes a selfie with him.*
She looks him up and down, looks at his clothes.

(Re. *his jacket*). Loving the drapes mate (*to the others*) look at the apparel! Cat-walk mate. Makes you lot look like bin-men.

DANNY (Re. *his own jacket*). What you talking about. This is genuine Paul Smith rip-off – (*touches his collar like it's scolding*) SSSSSSSSS – still hot (*laughs*).

SAMMY. Yea – goes well with your home-*broo* aftershave – odour-de-toilet.

All laugh.
MEGAN *smells* ARGY'S *neck.*

MEGAN. Chanel. Egoist? Fifty quid a splash. Am I right mate or am I right?

ARGY *smiles.*
SHELLY *shakes her head, disgusted at the opulence.*

Quality. I know my scent.

DANNY. You gonna do it for us then? Your song.

MEGAN. Give your man a break y' philistine, you hairy ball-scratcher – he's always got his hand on his balls him.

DANNY – *embarrassed* – *pockets his hands.*

SAMMY. Yea, what about it Argy? You gonna sing?

MEGAN. He's been yodelling all year y' brain-shy, he's resting his wriggling-throat (*to* ARGY) you're resting the tongue-talent ain't you mate?

DANNY. How do you know, he can speak for himself can't he –

MEGAN. The lad is swimming with the big fish mate, he ain't going to be singing to no pond-life outside a crappy working men's club is he?

DANNY *rifles around his pockets for money.*
He pulls out some small notes and coins.

DANNY. I've got the Doubloon. How much you charge?

MEGAN. He charges like a wounded buffalo mate that's how much he charges – (*Re.* DANNY'S *money*) put your job-seekers allowance away 'y benefits-thief – you ain't got enough there to pay for his coffee.

SAMMY. This is where he used to sing (*to* ARGY) this is where you used to sing.

SHELLY (*unkind*). He won't be opening his gob tonight. Not unless there's *a lot* money on the table – (*to* ARGY/ *mimicking* MEGAN) am I right *mate* or am I right?

MEGAN (*in* ARGY'S *defence*). I don't blame him, I'd rape it if I was on the big stage – anyway he's off-duty, you're off duty ain't you bab?

The world 'duty' triggers something in ARGY.
His face changes.
An anger falls across it.
He takes out his guitar.
They all cheer with delight.
He strums the opening bars of 'Technodanceaphobic.'
They all get excited.
Except for SHELLY.
She folds her arms and takes a step away from her brother.
ARGY *turns towards* SHELLY.
He looks her directly in the eye and sings 'Technodanceaphobic.'

Technodanceaphobic
https://www.youtube.com/watch?v=6WfVs6Vz52Q

ARGY
Shelly Was A Good Girl
She Never Left her Daddy's Side
She Was A Technodanceaphobic
And Every Night Inside She'd Cry

SHELLY *looks immediately emotional.*
ARGY *turns to* MEGAN, *looks at her and smiles.*
MEGAN *screams and whoops.*

ARGY
Megan Was A Bad Girl

MEGAN *claps excitedly and dances.*

ARGY
She Never Knew No Right From Wrong

Well They Found Her Alone
Her Daddy Left Her At Home
And Hoped That She Was Gone
Yeah Yeah

Everyone (except for SHELLY) *joins in the chorus.*

ARGY et al
Cuz' They Were Bangin' On The Back Seat All Night Long
Yeah They Were Bangin' On The Back Seat All Night Long
Yeah They Were Bangin' On The Backseat
On The Backseat
Bangin' On The Back Seat All Night Long

ARGY *turns to* SAMMY *now.*

ARGY
Sammy Was A Good Boy

SAMMY. Ha ha too good dude, I was too good

ARGY.
He Never Left His Mummy's Side

DANNY. He's a Mummy's boy (*laughs*).

ARGY.
He Was An Alcoholaphobic
And Every night Inside He'd Cry.

ARGY *turns to* DANNY.

We'll Live and Die in These Towns

ARGY
Danny was A Bad Boy

DANNY. Born bad!

ARGY
He Liked To Kick And Scream And Shout
Well On A Saturday Night, He Got The Feeling Alright
To Throw His Weight About Yeah Yeah.

ARGY (et al.)
Cuz' They Were Bangin' On The Back Seat All Night Long
Yeah They Were Bangin' On The Back Seat All Night Long
Yeah They Were Bangin' On The Backseat
On The Backseat
Bangin' On The Back Seat All Night Long
Yeah Yeah
So They Were Bangin' On The Back Seat All Night Long
Yeah They Were Bangin' On The Back Seat All Night Long
Yeah They Were Bangin' On The Backseat
On The Backseat
Bangin' On The Back Seat All Night Long
I Said
Bangin' On The Back Seat
Yeah On The Backseat
Bangin' On The Back Seat
(All Night Long)
Yeah They Were Bangin' On The Back
On The Back Seat
Bangin' On The Backseat
All night long!

When ARGY *finishes the song, everyone – high on the buzz – surround him adoringly, hugging, kissing, back-slapping and thanking him.*
Except for DANNY.
He balloons back and forwards menacingly in the background.
SHELLY *looks separate and sad, watching on.*
MEGAN *notices* SHELLY *and intuits that she perhaps might need a little private time with* ARGY.

MEGAN (*shouts*). Taxi! (*To* ARGY). Well mate, I won't lie, it has been legendary but…there is a town out there waiting for us, and it ain't going to set itself on fire is it mate.

She kisses ARGY *full and long on the lips.*

I'm in a song mate. I…am in a song. My life is complete.
SAMMY (*hugs* ARGY). How did you know (*Indicates drinking with a hand gesture*)? Don't answer.

SAMMY *hugs* ARGY *like he is never going to let him go.*
DANNY *walks forward aggressively.*
For a moment it looks as though he might hit ARGY.
Everyone goes quiet for a moment in nervous anticipation.
DANNY *leans forward so that his forehead is touching* ARGY'S *forehead.*
The silence that is palpable.
Eventually:

DANNY (*shouts*). Call the police!

Everyone looks momentarily confused.
DANNY *steps away from* ARGY.

We'll Live and Die in These Towns

DANNY'S *frown falls away and he smiles.*

(*Sings*). 'Cus things are gonna get ugly.

Everyone laughs and screams and whoops.
They get it.
DANNY *is singing the opening lines of* 'Aggro'.
DANNY *holds his hands out to* MEGAN *and* SAMMY.

(*Sings* **Aggro**).

Call the police
'Cus things are getting ugly
Get on your feet.

https://www.youtube.com/watch?v=Ct7FuFI9KzQ

They all hold hands.

(Sings). I want you running with me.

All three turn to face ARGY *as* DANNY *sings a few more lines from 'Aggro.'*

DANNY (*sings*).
Do what you like.
Say what you mean.
Do what you please.

DANNY/MEGAN/SAMMY. *(sing)*:
AHHH we'll set the streets on fire
And when it comes on top.
We'll give it lots of aggro

DANNY *et al. exit.*

AHHH we'll set the streets on fire
And when it comes on top.
We'll give it lots of aggro

They all disappear off stage.
Their song echoes in the air.
ARGY *is left alone with* SHELLY.
She looks sad.

ARGY. I suppose I'd better go.

He kisses her.
He hugs her very tightly.
He takes out a £50 note.
He offers it to her.

SHELLY. You don't have to give me money every time you see me. You always give me money.
ARGY. It ain't much Shell. Its only 50 quid.
SHELLY. £50 is a lot of money to me.

He forces it into her hand.
She does not offer much resistance.
She looks at the money, excited.

I can get my hair done.

ARGY *takes off his jacket and wraps it around her.*
She looks sorry now for her unkindness.

ARGY. Ah, Shell, I love you so much.

She is moved. She believes him.

SHELLY. Don't take any notice of me Argy. I don't even know what I'm saying half the time. (*Pause*) I tell everyone you're my brother you know. No one believes me. I don't even care.

(*A beat*).

We're all proud of you.

SHELLY *kisses and hugs him.*

You didn't abandon me.

A beat.

You didn't abandon our dad.

SHELLY *has tears running down her face.*

She ain't forgot about you. Jane. (*Pause*) She still talks to *me* y' know – I think she forgets I'm your sister.

He smiles sadly, he knows.

ARGY *walks away.*

(*After him*). You should sing to her.

ARGY'S *head drops...he keeps walking.*

Sing to her Argy. She'd like that.

We hear the melody of 'This Song' as ARGY *walks.*
A lighting change.
ARGY *is standing outside a derelict house.*
He is looking to the upstairs window.
He shakes his head as though old memories are flooding in.
He sits on the broken wall.
He starts the song slow and angry, and builds into a fast and frantic anger.

40 Days and 40 Nights.
https://www.youtube.com/watch?v=6iegJIU4IH0

ARGY.
I took a walk to the supermarket
It was so cold
I couldn't get back home
Through all the snow
Took A Vacation To The Petrol Station.
They Were Sold Out
I couldn't Get Back Home
They Didn't Want to Know.

(He speeds up to a frenzy)

Well, I was talking, lost in conversation, When you stopped in anticipation
You couldn't quite believe what you were hearing
And oh-whoa-oh-whoa-oh-oh-oh
But what I heard a little birdy told me
And what she said is quite serious

We'll Live and Die in These Towns

Well she told me you're sleeping with the enemy
Woah-woah-oh-woah-oh-oh-oh
She's at it all night long
Where did it all go wrong?
She's at it all night long
Long – yeahhh
40 days and 40 nights ohhh
One too many girlfriends
40 days and 40 nights ohhh
Who you gonna feed her
40 days and 40 nights ohhh
Now you gotta problem
40 days and 40 nights ohhh
What ya gonna do about that?
She's at it all night long
Where did it all go wrong?
She's at it all night long
Long…yeahhh
40 days and 40 nights ohhh
One too many girlfriends
40 days and 40 nights ohhh
What ya gonna feed her?
40 days and 40 nights ohhh
Now ya got a problem
40 days and 40 nights
What ya gonna do about that?
Ya just slack
What d'ya know about that?

A man (OWL) walks past as ARGY sings.
He is in a shabby suit.
He is talking urgently into a mobile phone.

He is carrying a briefcase.
The briefcase is handcuffed to his own wrist.
He is wearing a tie.
He sees ARGY and smiles – he clearly recognises him.

OWL *(into his ear piece)*. Got to go. Later...later...yea, yea, yea later. (*To* ARGY) Argy.

ARGY *sees OWL and immediately stops singing.*

ARGY. Owl!

ARGY *stands and hugs* OWL.

OWL. *Hello* – hugs as well.
ARGY. How are you?
OWL. You know. Ducking. Diving. Dealing.
ARGY (*Smiles/Re. tie*). Like the tie!
OWL (*embarrassed*). Yea well, opens doors don't it son, doors that would otherwise slam shut in your face. Got a big meeting with a noisy businessman from over the pond, as it goes. Doing a little labour for a multi-lingual, multi-faceted, multi-national – (*Re. house*) what you doing anyway? Dossing it ain't you, hanging round here, thought you was high-flying, papers said you'd got a slot on the big stage – The Throne Room or something.

ARGY *is clearly uncomfortable talking about the big gig.*

ARGY. I used to live here didn't I. Me and Jane. We had a room. (ARGY *points to upstairs window*). That one there – the window is *still* cracked, we used to freeze half to death in the winter, I had to sleep in a polo neck under three quilts.

OWL. Come a long way since then son – you could purchase ten houses like that now I bet, must be creaming it in.

ARGY *points to* OWL'S *suitcase, chained to his wrist.*

ARGY. Looks important.

OWL *hugs the briefcase protectively to his chest.*
He acts as though it contains the Crown Jewels.

OWL. It is important. Documentation ain't it. Transactions. Contracts. They'd mug you round here for your gold fillings. The police go around in threes – and that's inside the station (*laughs at his own joke*) No. If the fuckers want this baby, they'll have to hack my arm off for it.

ARGY (*Re.* OWL'S *business apparel*). This to do with the studio (*off* OWL'S *confused look*). You was going to set up a music studio? Last time we spoke...weren't you going to produce...local bands?

OWL. Oh yea – I'm still going to do that, eventually, that is still high on the agenda son, coin allowing, *coin allowing* – I was head-hunted wun I, by this guy (*taps suitcase*). 9-figure-company, the director recruited *me* personally – seduced me into the world of big business.

ARGY. You writing for them then – for this company, you back on the pen?

OWL. No, no this is, this is like –

OWL *takes a crumpled brochure from his pocket.*

I sacked the *song* a year ago, can't be doing with it, what I do now right is... we help people to earn laaaarge amounts of money. From home. I'm tired of being ripped off, I've *had it* with making other people money.
ARGY. So...nothing to do with –
OWL. There's no money in music, everyone's giving their song away for free on the World Wide Web, you can't make money –
ARGY. But it was...we was never really about the money, we was –
OWL. Yea, well *you* can say that, you've got coin –
ARGY. Only 'cus -
OWL *(interrupts)*. They'll shag you though won't they – the industry – they always do – the only way to make money these days is if you buy a printing press –

OWL *thrusts the brochure at* ARGY.

Have a gander at that.
ARGY *(looks)*. What is it?
OWL. Multi-level marketing.

ARGY *looks at the brochure.*

ARGY. Pyramid selling?
OWL (offended). No! Multi-level – *where does it say anything about pyramids?* Look *(points to brochure)* the company headquarters: New York, New York, Fifth Avenue – does that look like pyramid selling to you – it is legit, look, right next to the Trump Tower, I am talking serious coin, they've got like 700,000 *Action Takers* signed up worldwide.
ARGY. Action Takers?

OWL. It's mental – for an investment of $15 right, for an initial outlay of 15 crisp America $ you can make thousands a month *really quickly* –

ARGY (*doesn't buy it*). Really?

OWL. No *boring* early mornings, no dragging your feet along the pavement with *the weak and the feeble* – forgive the pun – begging for your slice of the working wage –

ARGY. Thousands a month for $15?!

OWL. (*Re. brochure*) Invest in this baby and you working day can be done by dinner time, feet up with a brew, watching day-time TV –

ARGY (in ironic jest). That sounds like a song.

OWL. There's no coin in song writing anymore, it's a closed shop, everyone knows that, it's all tied up ain't it, by the big publishing houses, they won't let anyone in –

ARGY. That's not really true though is it –?

OWL (*interrupts on 'true'*). All right, you've had a bit of luck. You got signed. That would not happen today – the tunes are all produced by teams in rooms, it's a conveyer belt churning out crap pop songs for the dumb masses – everyone says the same -

ARGY. Who's everyone?

OWL. The artist is dead Argy!

ARGY (*points to the house*). But –

OWL. What I'm going to do right, I'm gonna make my fortune on the markets, then, I can set up my own studio – financial independence allows you to be *innovatively free.*

ARGY. I wrote all my best songs right here, in that room (*Re House*). A Bic pen and a lined note pad from Pound-Land.

OWL. That was then. That was *a moment* Argy…that wouldn't happen today son. You wouldn't get through the door. The market has changed (*Re brochure*) this is *tomorrow.*

ARGY *sadly hands the brochure back to* OWL.

No, no, no you keep it, just in case: it's only a fifteen squid punt, then *you* get three people to pay you 15, then they get three people to pay them 15 – everyone knows three people right – and, *this is the exciting bit* (makes a cash sound) *kerching! You* get a cut of every $15 that rolls in – like I said it's a printing press.

ARGY'S *can't hide his sadness that his old friend has sunk to this.*
OWL *sees this, and takes the brochure back.*

Your loss son.
ARGY. Yea...anyway...I've...I'd better shoot.
OWL. Whatever.

He hugs OWL.

Listen, I know I shouldn't ask, I know I'm risking our friendship but...you couldn't throw a few squid in my direction could you, tide me over – the spondulies are bit tight – (*Re. brochure*) I've invested all my capital into the marketing.
ARGY. Yea, course, how much do you need?

ARGY *takes out his wallet.*

OWL. A couple of grand will see me through.
ARGY. Couple of grand!
OWL. Only till me ship comes in son – I'm expecting a cheque any day – anyway two k is loose-change to a bloke like you, you're clawing it in I heard.

ARGY. I haven't got two grand – I don't carry that kind of money round with me –
OWL. We could go to the cash-point –
ARGY. I'm off.

ARGY *starts to walk away, embarrassed, angry, and dissonant.* OWL *grabs his arm desperately.*

OWL. Don't walk away from me...my friend, my old friend. A grand then – 500.
ARGY. You're asking too much.
OWL. 200! That'll pay my rent.

ARGY *ignores him and walks.*

You forget where you come from fella – its people like me who put you where you are today, you should remember that.

ARGY *stops.*

ARGY. *People like you* what the fuck is that supposed to mean?
OWL. I came over from the Bullring. On the bus. Every day. Sat with you writing songs outside that greasy-spoon in town – we all did – drinking shit tea from cracked mugs, eating pot noodles and pork pies nicked from the petrol station *you forget*; and I nicked them, me, 'cus we had no money – you didn't even have enough coin to fill your bath with hot water.
ARGY. None of us had any money, we didn't care –
OWL. I waited for your call fella. I never got the call.
ARGY. What call?

OWL. Exactly. You get signed, the door to the kingdom opens for you...we don't get the call.
ARGY. So you think...it's my fault that you didn't break through?
OWL. Just saying.
ARGY. And I just had a lucky break?

OWL *shrugs as though this should be self-evident.*

OWL. Just being honest son.
ARGY. Nothing to do with the fact that I walked the streets with my strings for three years so I could earn enough money to buy some studio time. Nothing to do with the fact that I sent my demo tape to three hundred studios – two hundred and ninety-nine of them said 'fuck off you chancer! Leave your number in the bin.' I had my forty days and forty nights in the wilderness, *every* demon tempting me away from the song, *every* Satan...don't tell me I was *fucking* lucky...do you know how close my head came to breaking? I sacrificed everything for the song, everything, everything *fucking* everything.

A beat.

OWL. Yea. Well. We all heard about you and Jane. Maybe that's the difference between me and you Argy. I wouldn't sell my soul down the river. Not for a crappy record contract.

BANG!
ARGY *explodes and punches* OWL *in the nose.*
OWL *falls to the floor.*
OWL *feels his sore face.*

OWL (*arrogantly*). Law suit.

ARGY. Fill your boots y' twat. It'd be more honest than your crappy pyramid-scheme.

ARGY *walks away, and then walks back determinedly.*

I'll tell you what the difference is between me and you shall I? Shall I tell you? Do you really want to know why *you* didn't make it and *I* did *my friend, my old friend* – too much talking, too much blame, not enough time honing the talent, too much time feeling fucking sorry for yourself *and it was always someone else's fault wasn't it.* I did the work! You did not do the work. You didn't make it because you just didn't fucking want it enough. Just being honest son.

ARGY *takes £20 from his pocket.*
He thrusts it at OWL.

For the pot-noodles. For the pork pies.

ARGY *walks.*
He is emotional.
He looks as though he might implode at any moment.
The sky becomes very dark suddenly.
Storm clouds overhead.
Thunder, lightning, gales.
ARGY *walks.*
A heavy/dark fog falls.
The stage is almost black.
Disparate verses from his songs taunt him from out of the darkness.
ARGY *stops.*

Geoff Thompson

The verses burst angrily from every angle of the stage.
In front, behind, above, below, from the left, from the right.
ARGY balloons back and forward, as though trying to escape his own lyrics.
It is as though the songs are a sign of his growing mania.

(**Had Enough**).
Give me a good enough reason
why I should not cut you down.

(**You're Not Alone**).
Now in the street men stand in lines
They're all wasted anyway.

(**Aggro**).
Call the police
'cus things are gonna get ugly.

(**It's Not OK**).
Stop living your life for the man in a tie
He's just a fool the same as you.

(**Pressure**).
Pressure, pressure, step into the pressure zone.

(**40 Day and 40 Nights**).
40 days and 40 nights ohhh
Yeah you got a problem.

(**You're Not Alone**).
You sold us down the river like rats
Then you drowned and beat the brave.

We'll Live and Die in These Towns

Rain pisses down suddenly.
ARGY get soaked to the skin.
ARGY screams into the sky.

ARGY. You can fuck off as well!

(Beat)

What more do you want from me?

The music stops dead!
Stark silence.

What do you want!!! I am talking to you. Show your face you twat! You coward – show your face!

ARGY beats his fists on his chest.
Splays his arms challengingly.

I'm talking to you. Where are you???!!!

*Suddenly a large **12-foot crucifix** appears in front of him, miraculously, from out of the fog.*
It looks as though it is suspended in midair.
ARGY drops to his knees in terror.

What do you want?

*Out of the fog: **a booming voice**.*

BOOMING VOICE *(off)*. Keep going!

ARGY looks confused and scared. Is this the voice of God?

ARGY. What!?
BOOMING VOICE (*off*). Keep going. Don't stop.
ARGY (*still dissonant*). I don't (understand)...what?!!

The fog clears as suddenly as it appeared.
The crucifix is clearer now; it is hanging from a chain, attached to an overhead crane (that we do not necessarily see).
We see TWO WORKERS (*from the back*) *dressed in donkey jackets, standing underneath – and holding the bottom of – the crucifix, guiding it to a fixing point on the ground.*
We realise immediately that the booming voice belongs to WORKER 1 *who is talking to and directing an unseen crane driver.*
Behind them we see a sign: **The Phoenix Church.**

WORKER 1 (*to unseen crane driver*). Keep going, keep going (*hand out in a stop sign*) STOP! STOP!

The TWO WORKERS *firmly secure the crucifix in its fixing.*
ARGY *looks pale.*
WORKER 1 *turns and sees* ARGY *on his knees.*
WORKER 1 *has buck teeth and glasses.*
He can see that ARGY *is troubled.*

Oh my good God I am so sorry.

WORKER 2 *exits.*
WORKER 1 *holds out his hand and helps* ARGY *up.*

I didn't see you there. You could have been *crushed by the cross* – that would *not* have looked good in the Parish Chronicle. Are you all right? Were you looking for me?

ARGY *looks doubly confused.*
Why would he be looking for a random workman?
WORKER 1 *sees* ARGY'S *confusion.*

Ah! Sorry. Silly of me

He takes off his donkey jacket.
*He reveals his black shirt and **dog collar** underneath.*
He is a priest.
In fact, WORKER 1 *appears to be a sickly-sweet, archetypal, sock-and-sandals preacher.*

(Re. *collar*) I'm the local dog-collar.

WORKER 1 *notices* ARGY'S *guitar. He clocks his face.*

Aren't you… you're…you that wrote that song?

WORKER 1 *does a terrible, posh, middle class version of* 'Aggro.'

(Sings). 'I am going to set those streets on fire, and when things get on top, I am going to give it lots of aggro, I'll be giving it lots of aggro…'

ARGY *turns away from* WORKER 1, *stifling an astounded laugh.*

ARGY. For the love of God.
WORKER 1. Yes, well, perhaps not exactly as you envisioned it.

(Beat)

Can I help you? I was about to take a break if you'd like to chat.

ARGY *hesitates, shakes his head.*

I am sure you are very busy.

An uncomfortable impasse.
WORKER 1 *does not know what to say next.*
WORKER 1's *eyes light up: an inspiration.*
*He takes a **concert ticket** from his back pocket.*
He shows it to ARGY.

Front row seats. For your show. Tonight. The Throne Room Arena – I've been looking forward to it all year. (*Re. dog collar*) In plain clothes of course – I wouldn't want to scare the horses.

ARGY'S *face drops.*
WORKER 1 *notices this.*

It must be very challenging. Bringing your song back to the place of your birth, where everyone knows you.
ARGY. Everyone *thinks* they know you.

WORKER 1 *looks at the large crucifix.*

WORKER 1. They say that a prophet is not without honour.... except in his own town...except in his own home.

This really speaks to ARGY.
It is as though the priest has identified his exact worry.

ARGY. I wouldn't mind a chat. If that's OK?

WORKER 1 *smiles and indicates a small wall behind them.*
They both sit down on the wall.
Neither speaks for a second, each waiting for the other to initiate.
Eventually the priest breaks the impasse.

WORKER 1. I'm a big fan. I hear God in you.
ARGY (*dismissive*). I don't think so. I am full of...(*thinks of the appropriate word*) **weakness.**

WORKER 1 *smiles at this.*

WORKER 1. Well yes of course, God always works through perfect weakness.

Another impasse.
No one is speaking.
Eventually:

(*To* ARGY). Sometimes...when you talk...perhaps to a stranger...someone that is not going to judge...perhaps about nothing in particular...the answer to your problem presents itself...(*indicates the heavens*) without any apparent effort.
ARGY. I've got nothing to say really...
WORKER 1. Why not start with –
ARGY (*over him*). It's just that I feel so *fucking* afraid...I am afraid...**all the time**...afraid...and it makes me feel so *fucking* ashamed....(*an embarrassed pause*) sorry father. I swore.

A beat.

WORKER 1. And what is it that you are so...*fucking* afraid of?

ARGY. Everything, everything, everything.

WORKER 1. I've got all afternoon (ARGY *hesitates*). What you expose to light Argy...must itself become light?

'You're Not Alone' start playing in the background.
ARGY takes a deep breath, and then starts talking.
ARGY is animated: he is telling the priest his story.
WORKER 1 is listening intently.

THE AMBASSADOR *appears on a large screen (<u>left, and behind</u> ARGY/WORKER 1): he is at the* BACK DOOR *of a stadium-like building:* THE THRONE ROOM. *He is silently pacing, impatiently looking at his watch.*

BILL also *appears on a large screen (<u>right, and behind</u> ARGY/WORKER 1). He is standing high on a midnight roof, looking out at the 'breathing embers of the city, laid out before him like an exotic creature': we can see the see the cathedral, we can see the three spires, and the floodlit football stadium.*

You're Not Alone is sung by various members of the ENSEMBLE, *over* ARGY, *so we are not privy to what he is saying.*
As the song plays, different members of the ENSEMBLE *are spot-lighted on different sections of the stage.*
THE AMBASSADOR *and* BILL *stay on screen throughout the whole song.*

We'll Live and Die in These Towns

You're Not Alone.
https://www.youtube.com/watch?v=mpzOejM5CrU

HIPS.
Don't let the sun go down
On our empire
It's too much to waste.

SHELLY.
And don't let the walls
Come down round our empire.
It's too much to wave goodbye.

BUSKER.
We've been working for a long time
We've been fighting for a way.

MEGAN/ SAMMY/DANNY.
Now in the streets men stand in lines.
They're all wasted anyway

MEGAN
You live in an incestuous world
Where your conscience holds no weight.

OWL.
You sold us down the river like rats
Then you drowned and beat the brave.

BUSKER.
You're not alone, you know
You're not alone, you know

You're not alone at all
You're not alone, you know
You're not alone, you know
You're not alone at all

HIPS.
Don't let the sun go down
On our empire
It's too much to waste.

SHELLY.
And don't let the rains come down,
On our empire
It's too much to wash away.

MEGAN/SAMMY/DANNY.
We've been working for a long time
We've been fighting for a way.
Now in the streets men stand in lines
They're all wasted anyway.

MEGAN
You live in an incestuous world
Where your conscience holds no weight.

SHELLY.
You sold us down the river like rats
Then you drowned and beast the brave

COMPANY
You're not alone, you know
You're not alone, you know

We'll Live and Die in These Towns

You're not alone at all
You're not alone, you know
You're not alone, you know
You're not alone at all

OWL.
There's just too many dreams
In this wasteland
For you to leave us all behind

SHELLY.
There's just too many dreams
In this wasteland
For you to leave us all behind

COMPANY
There's just too many dreams in this wasteland
For you to leave us all behind
You're not alone, you know
You're not alone, you know
You're not alone at all
You're not alone, you know
You're not alone, you know
You're not alone at all

The song ends.
ARGY *stops talking.*
His head is bowed.
The left, back-screen darkens, THE AMBASSADOR *disappears.*
The right, back-screen darkens, BILL *disappears.*
All the other characters fall into darkness.

WORKER 1 (*the priest*) *sits back.*
He contemplates what ARGY *has shared with him.*
There is a long pause where no one speaks.
When WORKER 1 *speaks now, he is like a different man.*
Gone is the fluffy, socks-and-sandals priest.
He is now like a man possessed of the Holy Spirit.
His stature has grown.
He has gravitas.
His words are certain: his words are wise and weighty.

WORKER 1. Interesting. You're afraid. But you can't identify *exactly* what it is you are afraid of or indeed why...and that is creating a cognitive dissonance...*confusion*, you are confused...which ironically creates the feeling of more fear. (*Thinks and thinks*). It's not real of course. Fear is *not* real **but**. But – if you believe it, now then, if you believe it, if you offer it *breath* fear can become a mighty evil: it can steal your home, it can steal your mind, it *could* steal your life – every day a tormented soul throws itself under the wheels of a London Tube train because they listened to fear. What I have learned and what I know is this: there is only Love. Fear is the belief that Love is lost – it is like layers of muddy belief covering Love. That is why fear can be a good thing. If the world is your map Argy, then fear is the cross that marks treasure.

ARGY. I *really* don't know what I'm afraid of...that's what makes me feel so *insane*

WORKER 1 *becomes quiet and still.*
He turns his head slightly to the right.
It is as though he is accessing an unseen advisor.
He closes his eyes.

We'll Live and Die in These Towns

WORKER 1 *illuminates; subtly but definitely.*
He opens his eyes quickly.
He has fallen into a spiritual trance.
He lifts his finger in the air as emphasis.

WORKER 1. Identify the children. When you have identified the children, trace the children back to their mother. Once you have located the mother you have found the solution. Identify your fears. Trace your fears back the cause of your fears. When you have found the cause of your fears, you have found the cure.
ARGY. Do you mean...find what I am most afraid of?

WORKER 1 *leans forward to add weight to his next words.*
ARGY *leans forward to hear them.*

WORKER 1. Not *what are you most afraid of*, rather, who is it, **in you**...that is most afraid? (*Pause*) If you strike the Shepherd, the sheep **will** scatter.

A beat.

ARGY. Could I ask you something Father?
WORKER 1. Yes of course.
ARGY. Is God....? Do you think that God...? Could it be that...? (*Deep breath/emotion*) Is He punishing me? (*Voice cracking*) you know, for things. Things I might have done?

WORKER 1 *smiles, sad for* ARGY'S *palpable suffering.*

WORKER 1. May I ask *you* a question? (ARGY nods). Who is it that is asking?

A long silence, ARGY *is trying to make sense of the question. Large silhouettes slowly start to appear to* ARGY'S *right hand side, shapeless at first, and impossible to discern, but taking clearer form (as a large cemetery gate, myriad headstones – a graveyard) as the next three dialogues unfold, and a realisation crystallises in* ARGY'S *mind.*

ARGY. I don't understand.
WORKER 1. Well as far as I can see, there are two of you Argy (*taps his head*) in here. Both are talking, both are telling contrasting stories. One is talking Truth and one is telling lies. The Truth wants you to be free... the *untruth*, he is *very afraid*. He does not want you to be free. What happens next is wholly determined by which voice you decide listen to.
ARGY. How do I know which one is which?
WORKER 1. You can always tell the difference between Truth and the untruth Argy. Truth always wants to lead you to *the future*, which might feel a little unsure and a tad unsafe, but it is real and it is undeniable and it is right in front of you. The *untruth* on the other hand...he wants to drag you back to the past...which of course promises familiarity and comfort and control but... from my experience the past only exists in graveyards.

ARGY *stands suddenly.*
He looks to his right: the cemetery gate is clear now, the headstones: a graveyard.
It is as though he can see the cemetery, but the priest cannot.

ARGY. I need to go now.
WORKER 1 (*stands*). You have a date with The Throne Room.
ARGY. I have a date with Jane.

The priest smiles sadly.
This seems to move him.

ARGY. Thank you.
WORER 1 (*looks to the sky*). Not me.

As ARGY exits (stage right) the silhouettes fade from the screen.
WORKER 1 looks around him to make sure he is completely alone.
He picks up an imaginary electric guitar, feels it in his hands.
He plugs it into an imaginary amp.
We literally hear the screeching feedback from a real instrument.
With (exaggerated) air guitar he plays the light-hum of the opening cords to Aggro.
(NOTE: although the guitar is imaginary, the sound should be real)
The priest goes all rock-star and strums the heavy opening riff:
This time when the priest sings there is a real menace to his voice.

Aggro
https://www.youtube.com/watch?v=Ct7FuFI9KzQ

WORKER 1.
Blood on the streets,
You see the trouble happening
Get on your feet,
You see the crowds are gathering
Do what you like,
Say what you mean
Do what you please,
Ahhhhh we'll set the streets on fire

And when it comes on top
We'll give it lots of aggro
We're giving it lots of aggro

Suddenly the shadow of the crucifix falls on the priest.
He sees it and stops playing.
He drops his arms.
He looks up at the cross and smiles broadly.

WORKER 1. Please forgive the vanity My Lord. It's just... it's such a wonderful opening riff.

A lighting change.
ARGY *is before a gravestone: it is standing largely in shadow.*
We do not immediately know whose grave it is.
He looks sad.
His eyes are welling up.
As the light rises on the gravestone we see the name: **'JANE.'**
ARGY *takes out his guitar.*
ARGY sings *'Happy Birthday Jane.'*

Happy Birthday Jane
https://www.youtube.com/watch?v=CIJ8JncoASw

ARGY.
Good Mornin Jane,
Happy Birthday, Once Again,
What Would We Do,
What Would We do Without You
Without You
Wake Up The Sun is Shining,
Shining For You,

We'll Live and Die in These Towns

To Take All Your Troubles Away,
Just For A Day,
To Take All Your Troubles Away,
Just For A Dayyyyy,
For A Dayyy,
So Good Night Jane,
Happy Birthday Once Again,
Now What Will We Do,
What Will We Do Without You,
Without You,

An older woman JANE'S MUM *enters the cemetery.*
She is carrying flowers.

Wake Up The Sun is Shining,
Shining For You,
To Take All Your Troubles Away,
Just For A Day,
To Take All Your Troubles Away,
Just For A Dayyyyy,
For A Dayyy,

Happy Birthday,
Happy Birthday,
Happy Birthday,
Happy Birthday Jane

JANE'S MUM *stands behind* ARGY *as he sings.*
He is unaware of her presence.
She stands with her arms folded, as though in judgment of ARGY.

Happy Birthday,
Happy Birthday,
Happy Birthday Jane

Happy Birthday,
Happy Birthday,
Happy Birthday Jane

Happy Birthday,
Happy Birthday,
Happy Birthday Jane.

The song ends.
For a moment there is silence.
ARGY *speaks emotionally to the* JANE'S *grave.*

ARGY. I'm stuck on a mountain Jane. I'm too scared to go up. I'm too scared to go down. I'm too scared to stay where I am *I'm scared to be alive.* I'm not ready to be without you Jane. I'm...I'm not ready...(*chokes*) I'm not ready to be without you, I'm not ready...I want to go back to how we was...I want to go back to *before*...

ARGY *breaks down weeping for the first time*
JANE'S MUM *unfolds her arms.*
She softens.
She is deeply moved by ARGY'S *words.*

JANE'S MUM. You can't go back.

ARGY *turns.*

We'll Live and Die in These Towns

There is no *before*.

ARGY looks startled to see JANE'S MUM *for the first time. He looks immediately nervous.*

None of us can go back, I wish we could, I wish *I* could.

A beat.

You think you left her. (ARGY'S *head drops*) you made a choice to follow your song and you think that means you left her…you never left her. She just didn't choose to come with you.

JANE'S MUM *puts the flowers on* JANE'S *grave*.

This (*the grave*) is not what you would have wished for her. This is not what I would have wished for *anyone*. But this was not your choice, this was not my choice…this was Jane's.

A beat.

ARGY. Do you hate me?

The question moves her almost to tears.
She is too choked to answer; she just shakes her head sadly.

(*Guilt*) I didn't send her a card and I feel –

JANE'S MUM (*emotional*). Don't you think we all feel racked? Because we didn't return her texts quickly enough, because we talked to her instead of listening, do you think I don't **hate** myself... (*she is very emotional/nearly crying*)... because I was too *bloody* busy with my very important life to notice *any* of the signs? (*Pause/settles herself*) She *did not* kill herself because you didn't send her a card on her birthday. (*Pause*) No one could have seen this coming. I didn't see it coming and I gave birth to her.

ARGY. I just want to be back on the settee in my little flat with her, combing my fingers through her hair *talking about us being free*...I should have stayed.

JANE'S MUM. And what would have happened if you'd stayed? For the first few months you would have both been happy. After a year, Jane would have encouraged you to *keep writing* and *keep singing* but... *get a job,* in an office, in a warehouse. After the second year she would have convinced you that a mortgage was a good idea – safety, security, she would have told you what me and her dad told *her*: rent is dead money, it makes no sense economically to pay rent when you can invest your earnings in a mortgage. Jane could be very convincing. You would have felt certain that you could work a job, and pay a mortgage and still chase your song. After three years, the song would stop calling you. Then you would start to resent Jane *because it was her that made you choose*. Then the arguments. Then the rows. Every morning you would wake up next to Jane suspecting that it was her fault your song was lost. And every morning Jane would wake up next to you, knowing that this was true.

ARGY *shakes his head, still upset.*

Nothing in this world comes without a price.

ARGY (*emotional*). It asks too much from me.

JANE'S MUM *looks at* ARGY *with great compassion.*

JANE'S MUM. No Argy. It asks *everything* of you.

She steps forward.
She touches ARGY'S *face tenderly, lovingly.*

But what it asks of you lovey, it has already taken. Can't you see that? You have already paid? And if you don't take what you paid for, that *would* be a waste.

She looks at JANE'S *grave.*

Then this really would have *all* been for nothing.

ARGY *breaks down and sobs.*
Years of mourning coming out all at once.
JANE'S MUM *hugs him tightly, shushes him.*
Eventually, they release the embrace.
ARGY *wipes the tears from his face.*

She loved you.
ARGY. She said she didn't.
JANE'S MUM (*Smiles*). She loved you *very* much.

ARGY *takes a deep breath: so much emotion.*
We hear the distant roar of 20,000 voices.
ARGY *and* JANE'S MUM *look towards the roars.*
After a moment:

The future is calling you.

A stark lighting change.
The roar gets louder and louder and louder.

Lights up.
A 20,000 strong crowd appear on the screen.
ARGY *is on stage at The Throne Room.*
ARGY'S *band are behind him,* YUDI, MATT, *and* KUSI *and* BRAHMA – *they are facing the crowd (his back to the theatre audience).*
THE AMBASSADOR *is stage left watching happily.*
Stage right we see BILL, JANE'S MUM, SHELLY *and* BUSKER.
ARGY *sings 'We'll Live and Die in These Towns.'*

We'll Live and Die in These Towns
https://www.youtube.com/watch?v=7miErQzz4Y8

ARGY.
You spend your time in smoky rooms
Where haggled old women
With cheap perfume say
It never happens for people
Like us you know
Well nothing ever happened on its own
And well the toilets smell of desperation
The streets all echo of aggravation
and you wonder.
Why you can't get no sleep.
When you've got nothing to do,
And you've had nothing to eat.

We'll Live and Die in These Towns

Your life's slipping
And sliding right out of view
And there's absolutely nothing
That you can do well

ARGY *and the* BAND *all turn away from the 20,000.*
They turn and face the theatre audience.
The ENSEMBLE *joins* ARGY *on stage.*
They all sing the chorus.

ARGY (et al).
We'll live and die,
We'll live and die in these towns
Don't let it drag you down
Don't let it drag you down now
We'll live and die,
We'll live and die in these towns
Don't let it drag you down
Don't let it drag you down now
Dirty dishes from a TV meal
That went cold from the wind
Through a smashed up window
You can't go out if anybody calls ya
Cos you can't have a bath
When there's no hot water
And your friends are out
On the town again.
And you ask yourself if it will ever end
And it's all too much for your head to take.
Just a matter of time
Before you break, well
We'll live and die

We'll live and die in these towns
Don't let it drag you down
Don't let it drag you down now
We'll live and die,
We'll live and die in these towns
Don't let it drag you down
Don't let it drag you down now

Now...
Now...

We'll live and die,
We'll live and die in these towns
Don't let it drag you down
Don't let it drag you down now
We'll live and die,
We'll live and die in these towns
Don't let it drag you down
Don't let it drag you down now

ARGY *and the ensemble break straight into* ***'You're Not Alone.'***

ARGY.
Don't let the sun go down
On our empire
It's too much to waste.
And don't let the walls
Come down round our empire.
It's too much to wave goodbye.
We've been working for a long time
We've been fighting for a way.
Now in the streets men stand in lines.

We'll Live and Die in These Towns

They're all wasted anyway
You live in an incestuous world
Where your conscience holds no weight.
You sold us down the river like rats
Then you drowned and beat the brave.
You're not alone, you know
You're not alone, you know
You're not alone at all
You're not alone, you know
You're not alone, you know
You're not alone at all
Don't let the sun go down
On our empire
It's too much to waste.
And don't let the rains come down,
On our empire
It's too much to wash away.
We've been working for a long time
We've been fighting for a way.
Now in the streets men stand in lines
They're all wasted anyway.
You live in an incestuous world
Where your conscience holds no weight.
You sold us down the river like rats
Then you drowned and beat the brave
You're not alone, you know
You're not alone, you know
You're not alone at all
You're not alone, you know
You're not alone, you know
You're not alone at all

Yeah...
Not alone not alone
There's just too many dreams
In this wasteland
For you to leave us all behind
There's just too many dreams
In this wasteland
For you to leave us all behind
You're not alone, you know
You're not alone, you know
You're not alone at all
You're not alone, you know
You're not alone, you know
You're not alone at all

ARGY and *the ensemble break straight into the finale **'This Song.'***

ARGY.
Half the kids that you grew up with
Were pushing prams by the time that they were just sixteen
If love is a drug then where is the cure
For the girl who used to talk to you about her dream
And all the boys with all their toys
Couldn't see the signs as we scorched out eyes with nicotine
And the grown-ups said listen to your heads
But our hearts were crying out for heroes on TV screens
Now this song is about you
Now this song is about...
Changes in your mind
Changes in your lives
Changes in the times
And the reason you can't sleep at night

Changes in your mind
Changes in your lives
Changes in the times
And the reason you gave up the fight
Half the kids that aren't pushing prams
Are now pushing pills to boys and girls who are half their age
And the pubs and clubs are full of drunks
Who don't remember the day they were born or even remember their names
An old man sings a tune he knew but he's drowned out by a fight next to a fruit machine
And all of this, our hearts, our nation
Total lack of civilization
Will it ever be the same?
Now this song is about you
Now this song is about…
Changes in your mind
Changes in your lives
Changes in the times
And the reason you won't sleep tonight
Changes in your mind
Changes in our lives
Changes in the times
And the reason we gave up the fight
Now this song…is about, is about, is about you (x8)

END

GRAPHIC DESIGN
BRANDING
WEB DESIGN
MARKETING

CREATE ◩
ONSIGHT

DESIGN
FOR
THEATRE
AND
THE
ARTS

WWW.CREATEONSIGHT.CO.UK